HOPE IN THE GRIND

90 DAYS OF BIBLICAL ENCOURAGEMENT FOR FAITH, WORK, AND LIFE

MATT CLARKE

with

SHERRI GRAGG

CONTENTS

DEDICATION

I dedicate this book to my amazing wife, who pulls out of me every day the man that God created me to be; to Jesus Christ, to whom I owe everything; and to everyone who wakes up in the morning and, with calloused hands and faithful hearts, grinds out a life that God can be proud of by the sweat of their brow.

ACKNOWLEDGMENTS

I would like to thank Susan, my wife, best friend, and chief encourager in all things, for the patience and love she has shown me—not only through this project but through all the grind of real life behind its stories.

To Mike Hardwick, my mentor and friend, thank you for decades of pouring into me as a leader and a man as I continue to figure things out.

To Andy Andrews and Dave Ramsey, thank you for the advice and encouragement to put a book together and for your wisdom on how to do it well.

To Sherri Gragg, thank you for seeing the vision and taking a collection of daily writings and doing the difficult work of compiling and editing them into book form.

To Elicia Hyder, thank you for holding my hand and shepherding me through the process of creating and publishing this book and for bringing it to life.

To the countless friends across the industry who encourage me daily to keep writing—your support means more than you know.

To my team and colleagues at Churchill Mortgage, your support every day has enriched my life in extraordinary ways.

To my family and friends who experience the messy daily grind by my side and love me anyway.

And finally, to my 15½-year-old golden retriever, Louie, who is not only the subject of many of my writings but my faithful writing partner. He lay beside me in the dark early mornings every day while I pondered my thoughts, wrestled with God, and put words to what came out.

WHAT OTHERS ARE SAYING

"Mix an intense Will Rogers with a great Bible story teller and you have my friend Matt. These pages will lift you and instruct you like they have me. Settle in on the back porch or in front of a good fire and enjoy the read and the ride."

DAVE RAMSEY, BESTSELLING AUTHOR

"*Hope in the Grind* speaks to the sacred work of showing up every day. Author Matt Clarke skillfully reminds us that faith isn't found apart from the grind—it's forged inside it. Delivered with clarity, humility, and a touch of wry humor, *Hope in the Grind* contains timely, practical wisdom for anyone trying to live faithfully where life actually happens."

ANDY ANDREWS, NEW YORK TIMES BESTSELLING AUTHOR OF THE TRAVELER'S GIFT AND THE NOTICER

"Finally, a daily devotional guide written from the gritty, trenches of real life! Matt Clark has been there. He's a successful business leader, a devoted husband and father, and a good friend. But he's also walked through dark seasons, navigating divorce, addiction, and the madness of business leadership.

In this outstanding daily devotional guide, Matt walks alongside the reader—he doesn't wave a finger at us—and invites us to experience the lessons and impact of the real-life stories of scripture and the chaotic world unfolding all around us, in raw and honest ways. He offers a framework of six core convictions to help readers live better in all facets of our lives, while always remaining tethered to the one, true source of peace.

There are no cliches to be found, and no soul-less tropes to wallpaper over how hard living life as a person of faith truly can be. Matt's voice is refreshing, honest, and insightful, calling everyone—from the exhausted father, the burdened mother, and the anxious business leader - into daily reflections and challenges to live fuller, God-centered, and successful lives.

This devotional guide is a must-read—and a book that you will return to over and over again in times of great challenge and sorrow, and in seasons of great joy and success."

DR. JOHN DELONY, BESTSELLING AUTHOR
AND SPEAKER

"*Hope in the Grind* is one of those rare books that meets you exactly where you are—right in the middle of real life. Matt Clarke doesn't write from a pedestal; he writes from the trenches. With honesty, humility, humor, and deep faith, he reminds us that God shows up not just in the quiet moments, but in the chaos, the struggle, the work, and the becoming.

Matt's story is powerful because it's relatable. He invites you into a journey marked by grit, grace, redemption, and purpose. This book is a reminder that God uses imperfect people to do meaningful work.

For anyone leading a family, a business, a team, or simply trying to live a life of intention and integrity, *Hope in the Grind* is an encouraging, grounding, and deeply human read.

I have followed Matt's journey for years and believe that this book will strengthen your faith, steady your leadership, and remind you that hope is always available—especially in the grind."

CINDY ERTMAN, FOUNDER AND CEO, THE DEFINING DIFFERENCE®, MORTGAGE INDUSTRY LEADER AND COACH

"Matt Clarke radiates hope and light. Always. It's because he believes in and walks in the light of Christ. John Wesley said, 'Light yourself on fire with the passion of Christ. And people will come from miles around just to watch you burn.' That's why when Matt speaks.I listen."

CHAPLAIN JERRY LEACHMAN

"I've had the privilege of knowing Matt Clarke for more than two decades—both as a colleague and as a personal friend. When I first hired Matt at Churchill Mortgage, he had no prior mortgage banking experience, but it was immediately clear that he possessed the character, drive, and humility that would carry him far. Over the years, I have watched him grow into an exceptional mortgage professional, a respected leader, and a man deeply grounded in faith.

Beyond our professional journey, my relationship with Matt has become one of the great blessings of my life. I've grown to truly love, appreciate, and respect him, his amazing and equally talented wife Susan, and their wonderful family. We've shared countless memories together over the past 2 decades—many business conferences, seminars, vacations and moments that have made us more like family than colleagues. In many ways, Matt feels like one of my own kids, and I couldn't be prouder of the man, husband, father and leader he's become.

Hope In The Grind reflects the heart and spirit of the Matt Clarke I know—authentic, compassionate, and unwavering in his faith. This daily devotional offers wisdom and encouragement for anyone walking through life's challenges, reminding us that perseverance, hope, and faith are the keys to turning adversity into growth. It will become a staple in my devotional library!"

MIKE HARDWICK, AUTHOR AND FOUNDER
OF CHURCHILL MORTGAGE CORPORATION
AND MULTIPLE OTHER FINANCIAL SERVICES
COMPANIES

"For the last couple of decades, I've watched Matt Clarke show up and do all the things you'll read about in these pages. These are practical daily stories, that if applied to your life, will make you a better spouse, parent, co-worker, teammate, employee, boss, leader and follower and you'll leave the world a better place for your having been here.

Matt doesn't just talk about his Core Convictions, he lives them out with incredible consistency day by day. You can trust what he has to say because you can trust him. If you're interested in having a legacy and executing each day with an eternal perspective in mind, keep reading!"

JIM MCQUAIG, BUSINESS OWNER AND
ENTREPRENEUR

Our world desperately needs and longs for voices of wisdom—true Sages who guide us with keen insight and grace. My very good friend and longtime trusted business associate, Matt Clarke, is one of those rare individuals. His life reflects a depth of understanding and a heart for others that makes him a role model exceedingly worthy of following. In your hands is a daily devotional unlike any other—a heartfelt collection of stories and lessons drawn from Matt's real-world experiences, shared honestly and vulnerably. Over 90 days, you'll discover practical guidance infused with hope and wisdom that can transform your life, family, relationships, and work. I highly recommend Matt and his powerful devotional.

CECIL O. KEMP JR., BUSINESS OWNER, LIFE COACH, LEADERSHIP MENTOR, AND AWARD-WINNING AUTHOR

"Matt's *Hope in the Grind* proves that true stability comes from not only grounding your career in what Matt calls his 'Core Convictions' but most importantly, Jesus Christ. Matt's daily devotions provide a true compass for leaders that want to transform their corporate chase into a meaningful spiritual mission. His devotionals are grounded in biblical truths that will guide anyone seeking to integrate faith with high-level excellence."

STEVE HAGEN, HEAD COACH, NFL ACADEMY INTERNATIONAL

"There are several reasons for you to have and hold on to Matt's collection of thoughts. Not only do the ideas from this book represent a genuine connection to the heart of so many topics, but they also reflect his discipline and commitment to doing his best to leave the world a better place. Matt's ability and willingness to connect a scriptural truth to a real-life scenario is truly remarkable, deeply inspiring and frankly so much of what our modern world needs in this moment. It's amazing when you read something daily and sometimes you laugh, sometimes you cry and other times you simply cherish the integration of the realities in our world to what scripture was meant to touch.

Much less of a book, I would say, and much more a gift from Matt. May this work impact you as it has so many over time. Matthew, well done good and faithful servant."

STEVE SCANLON, FOUNDER AND CEO OF
REWIRE, INC., AUTHOR, AND COACH

"I have been reading Matt's daily writings for years now. I always know that I will finish each one with new insights, a deeper perspective, as well as a new spiritual understanding. His discipling wisdom has made me a better man."

JIMMY YEARY, AWARD-WINNING
SONGWRITER AND SPEAKER

A NOTE FROM MATT CLARKE

I wasn't raised in church. I'm no great theologian, teacher, or minister. I never dreamed I'd write a devotional book. But I did, and I want you to experience the same hope that I do during the daily grind of everyday life.

Thank God he uses even those of us not qualified.

My journey of faith began when my children were little. I decided they should probably go to church, and I volunteered to serve in the children's ministry. One day, as I was pretending to teach, it occurred to me that I'd never actually read the Bible.

Guess I should start, I thought. So, I did. And I've read it every day since.

My day job is to serve as president of Churchill Mortgage, an employee-owned independent mortgage banker—which means we fight every day to thrive (or survive) without the backdrop of a bank or the public. We fight for families and for each other's success, every day. We grind.

I am a guy who is madly in love with his wife, who adores his children most days and wants to strangle them others. I am a person who has gone through divorce and serious illness and dealt with addiction and most curveballs life can throw—including brokenness and reconciliation within my own family.

I've experienced some super highs and painful lows, made a little money, lost a *lot* of money, been hired for jobs I didn't deserve, and been fired unexpectedly from others.

I've played sports, coached sports, and love everything related to sports in Boston. Unfortunately, I've even spent a few nights in jail—most after some really fun events, but once, after a really stupid one!

I did not grow up in church. Neither was I familiar with the Bible. Instead, I discovered both much later in life. I was, however, blessed with wonderful parents who loved me completely, and I knew it. I am super thankful because I'm aware that not everyone was as fortunate.

I've lived life just like many others, maybe even you. I get up and grind every day.

All that to say, I've learned something very important. God gave us all a voice to be used without shame, a voice that can either help others or hurt them. And how we choose to use our voice matters greatly.

In the pages that follow, I reference several experiences from my work at Churchill. Being a part of that company has truly changed my life. I can honestly say that it helped me discover the abundantly powerful love of God and the scandalous grace of Jesus.

Churchill's founder, Mike Hardwick, has been one of the

most spectacular mentors of my life. He loved me like a son and poured into me in ways I never expected. His parents started a church in Nashville when they were just eighteen years old. They also got married and pregnant with Mike right about that same time. Now, I don't know about you, but I could barely remember to change my underwear and brush my teeth at eighteen, let alone take care of someone else. If there wasn't a ball to kick, a beer to drink, or a blonde to chase, I wasn't interested. Mike's parents, however, built Christ Church Nashville into what most consider the first mega-church in the city, led by great teaching and a world class choir.

The Hardwicks were pastors in every sense of the word and wise business leaders, as well. Of course, Mike got a front-row seat, and what he learned was eventually poured into Churchill Mortgage. As God would direct it, what Mike learned was also poured into me.

Through the years, I've been blessed to have exposure to and friendships with some incredible people. These are people I consider giants in this world, and they have impacted me greatly. They are men and women who have stepped into my life and become mentors, many who have done so unknowingly.

I must say that I am constantly amazed at how God has taken this smart-mouthed kid from Massachusetts, a young man with an attitude greater than his ability to back it up, and placed him at the feet of so many great people. And most importantly, at the feet of Jesus.

Back in 2009, my friend and coworker Kevin McQuaig came into my office one day and said, "We should go on a mission trip."

"Sure," I replied, without actually knowing what a mission trip was.

I had, however, learned something critical throughout the years and it was this: nobody ever accomplished anything by saying no. On the other hand, memories are made, friendships developed, businesses built, and lives changed by saying yes (but don't forget to keep a *no* in your back pocket).

Soon after the invitation, off we went to Guatemala and

Haiti. Wow! Talk about an eye-opener. The poverty, the disease, the hardships and living conditions we encountered were overwhelming—almost as overwhelming as the joy that shone through it all.

As of the writing of this book, I've now led seventeen more trips to Guatemala, Haiti, and Honduras. We've built houses, schools, clinics, roads, churches, community centers, wells, and, probably most importantly, latrines. The impact you can have on a family by providing a sanitary place to go to the bathroom is hard to describe.

I led those trips because someone had to. Knowing that people are silently begging to be led, I wondered, Why not me? Each of these experiences has left me a better person.

Years ago, when Mike began to turn over the leadership responsibility of Churchill to me, I had to decide what kind of leader I would become. Following in the wake of a man who was adored by the company, the industry, and the community was a daunting task.

I decided that I could linger in Mike's shadow or create my own, which was what got me started down the pathway of the core convictions we will discuss in the following chapters. These are beliefs by which I want to operate every area of my life—family, work, and business.

They would, I decided, become guideposts that would lead me through whatever I was facing, principles I could both teach and be accountable to. I discovered that without them, the world would define me in a way that would never be good enough.

As you read the following chapters, I urge you to consider this carefully: God created you with purpose, with a spirit of power and love and with a sound mind. Therefore, live your life in that way.

In summary, I'm just a man who loves his wife, tequila, and Jesus (but not in that order), a man who started writing years ago in order to share his thoughts to our company as it grew. I figured that if the organization ever grew beyond my ability to know each teammate personally, then I could at least make sure they knew me.

That's how trust is built. And that is why I started writing each morning and began living my life out loud. At first, I shied away from too much Scripture, but soon I realized that was crazy. The Bible, I knew, sheds a bright, clear light on life, whether or not you believe in Jesus. The Bible is rich in direction, love, truth, and grace. These were things I was aware we *all* needed, which is the very reason I now share God's Word boldly.

Every day before I leave the house, I know I have three jobs: to fall head over heels in love with my Savior, to fall head over heels in love with my wife, and to fall head over heels in love with who my heavenly Father is shaping me to be. It's been my daily journey for a while. And now you are a part of it, too.

Welcome aboard. Thank you for joining me.

Matt Clarke
Nashville, Tennessee

Each morning, I write and send a daily devotional based on my own Bible readings. This book is a collection of those messages. You can subscribe to get new posts for free.

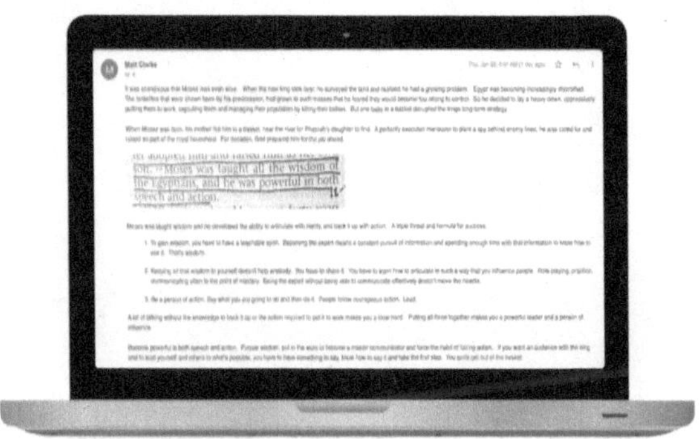

The original daily emails contain photographs of my actual Bible—the Every Man's Bible, New Living Translation, published by Tyndale. Due to copyright concerns, we've been unable to use the photos in this book.

I believe the Bible is meant to be consumed—torn up, chewed on, and swallowed, just as Jesus instructed John in Revelation. That means highlights, notes, dates, questions, and underlines.

When I write my daily reflections, I include the underlined

referenced verses because I believe there is something sacred about reading God's Word in God's Book, and I want to bring that experience into my thoughts and writings as much as possible.

Join today at www.dailygrindemail.com or scan this QR code with your phone's camera.

DRIFT AWAY
CORE CONVICTIONS

In 1973, Dobie Gray released his biggest hit, "Drift Away"[1]. While the chorus is certainly catchy, there's a message in one of the verses that I just can't get out of my head.

He sings of his fear that he's just wasting time, and like the apostle Paul, doesn't understand so many things he does. He laments how unkind the world appears and calls out for help to be carried through.

To stop the *drift*.

These sobering lyrics ring true in so many lives and businesses. Drifting is a slow, subtle departure from a set of standards, expectations, or values that happens over time. If we don't intentionally define our standards, we are in danger of drifting away from what matters most to us before we even know it is happening.

> **So we must listen very carefully to the truths we have heard, or we may drift away from them.**
>
> HEBREWS 2:1 (TLB)

Years ago, I wrote out a set of core convictions that set a standard for how I want to live my life. Now, they also serve as a guideline for how we operate our business at Churchill Mortgage.

1. I was created to serve others without exception.
2. Be the expert.
3. Be the hardest-working person in the room.
4. Leave people better for the encounter.
5. Do the next right thing.
6. Mornings matter.

Have you ever taken the time to write out your own core convictions? Doing so and clearly communicating those convictions to your team will profoundly affect your leadership, as it acts as a definition of what you expect from yourself and others. It will also serve as a filter for who you allow to join your team. After all, if you accept that belief systems are so strong that people simply cannot operate against them, why would you want people on your team who don't share your most important beliefs?

Where are you and your team drifting because you need to have stronger agreements on clear standards and goals? Take the time to define what you truly believe and establish guiding principles for your life and business.

Father, give me wisdom and clarity as I choose the core convictions that will guide my life and business.

CORE CONVICTION ONE
SERVE OTHERS WITHOUT EXCEPTION

I believe I was created to serve others without exception. Years ago, when I first began to formulate this core conviction, I wrote down, "I was created to serve others." I had to add "without exception" later. Those words transform the statement from a wish to a commitment, from something I hope to do to something *I am going to do*. Before I added those two little words, I found myself trying to decide who was worthy of my service. Then I realized that another person's worthiness is not my call to make.

Mark Worthington, a Churchill leader out West, knows this well. He and his wife, Carla, volunteer at a school they helped start in Igalaza Village, Uganda. The organization, Carla Christian School, provides impoverished children with an education and fresh drinking water.

He sat down and called them around him and said, "Anyone wanting to be the greatest must be the least —the servant of all!"

MARK 9:35 (TLB)

Each one of us can impact our communities and the world if we just have the courage to do so. This is true even if we don't think we can be of use or the timing just doesn't seem right. We have already been given everything we need to help others, and once we start, more provision will show up at just the right time.

Some of us don't feel we have what it takes to make a difference, but the Bible is filled with examples of times when God used seemingly incapable people:

- Gideon lacked stature and courage; God made him a warrior.
- Rahab was a prostitute; God used her to save Joshua's spies.
- Timothy was far too young; God used him to lead a church.
- Moses was afraid of public speaking; God equipped him to lead the Israelites to freedom.
- Peter was a head case; God called him the rock upon which he would build his church.

Whether in big ways, like volunteering for a trip to Uganda, or small ways, like bringing food to a homeless shelter, you have what you need to make a difference. Don't forget, the Bible says that to be the leader of any, you must be the servant of all (Matthew 20:26).

What is one way you can help meet someone else's needs today?

Father, show me how to serve others without exception today.

CORE CONVICTION TWO
BE THE HARDEST-WORKING PERSON IN THE ROOM

I know the adage "It's not whether you win or lose, it's how you play the game" is an important perspective to have, but I want to be around people who play to win.

Competition is natural. Even Jesus's disciples were competitive, vying for who was the greatest. In a great example of *unhealthy* competition, James and John brought their mother into the contest, hoping she could convince Jesus to crown her sons as the champs. When we are consumed by being better than the next guy, we chase an ever moving target. Often, that target isn't anywhere close to what we are capable of, and once we hit it, we are in danger of settling for something less than our best.

> **Pay careful attention to your own work, for then you will get the satisfaction of a job well done, and you won't need to compare yourself to anyone else. For we are each responsible for our own conduct.**
>
> GALATIANS 6:4–5

When God looks at you, he isn't comparing you to your neighbor to see who is better. He is looking to see what you did with the gifts he gave you. That is why my second core conviction is to be the hardest-working person in the room. Hard work is a virtue. It is not just what we do that matters but how we do it. No matter where we are or what task is before us, honoring God means executing with everything we have.

No matter what I am doing, I want to give it my all every day. I never want to create slack for somebody else to pick up. Lazy people get in the way. I want to be surrounded by other people who want to be the hardest-working people in the room, as well. That builds great momentum and creates unbelievable energy. When we focus on being our best every day, we encourage and empower our teammates to do the same.

Pay attention to your own work, and get the satisfaction of a job well done. Be the hardest-working person in the room.

Father, grant me the discipline, strength, and courage to be the hardest-working person in the room today.

CORE CONVICTION THREE
BE THE EXPERT

During one of my mission trips to Guatemala, we built concrete block homes as teams of local experts swarmed around us, directing every step. I learned a new skill along the way, so I figured I would unleash that skill at home.

I had an area on my property where I wanted a nice stone patio. Since I was cheap, willing to do hard work, and now an expert mason, it seemed like a perfect DIY opportunity. After a long weekend of hard work, it was mission accomplished. The patio looked good, and I felt like I might just have a new side hustle!

By the time spring rolled around, however, water puddled in all sorts of places, and stones were falling off around the edges. I realized that while I was becoming a tradesman in Guatemala, I forgot to appreciate the work the experts did alongside those of us who were amateurs that made the projects succeed. I approached my DIY project with blind ignorance, deceiving myself that I knew what I was doing.

And it showed.

> **Whatever you do, do well, for in death, where you are going, there is no working or planning, or knowing, or understanding.**
>
> ECCLESIASTES 9:10 (TLB)

This is a great example of why I developed my third core conviction, be the expert. Being the expert means that you strive to achieve a level of expertise in all you do through constant development of your skills and continued learning. If you look around my office and home, you will see books everywhere. I am constantly trying to feed my mind so that I can be a better leader, coworker, husband, and parent. Working hard without the humility to develop your skills makes you a hard-working amateur who is prone to mistakes and missed opportunities.

Since you cannot be the expert at everything, it is not a journey you can take alone. You must have the humility to surround yourself with people who are better than you. You also need mentors, experienced people who are achieving the results to which you aspire and who care enough to tell you the truth. Learn from them, and then apply the hard work and discipline to reach your goals.

Become the expert.

Father, lead me to the resources and mentors I need to be the expert.

5

CORE CONVICTION FOUR
LEAVE PEOPLE BETTER FOR THE ENCOUNTER

After finishing up a day of meetings, my son, Ethan, and I decided to run to the driving range. While I was swinging away, demonstrating for all to see that I was not created to play golf, an employee named Brian, who some would consider socially awkward, walked over and called Ethan by name. The two embraced like old friends.

It was clear that Brian made it a point to know as many people as possible as he was filling up the buckets of practice balls. When I joined them, Ethan introduced us, and that was it. Brian and I were now friends. We talked, laughed, and discussed Ethan's swing. Brian encouraged Ethan while watching him hit a few drives. And, when it was a bad shot, he was brutally honest while remaining kind. Brian was simply remarkable.

I couldn't help thinking about him while I was reading Matthew 9. Jesus heals a paralyzed man, recruits Matthew to the team, hangs out with a bunch of outcasts, heals a woman who had suffered for twelve years, brings a girl back to life, gives a blind man his sight, launches multiple rebukes at some self-righteous dudes, and travels around helping everyone he comes into contact with.

So encourage each other to build each other up, just as you are already doing.

1 THESSALONIANS 5:11 (TLB)

This is why my fourth core conviction is to leave people better for the encounter. Every interaction with another person is an opportunity to leave them better than you found them.

Everybody is dealing with things beneath the surface. Don't add on to it. Instead, take some of that burden. Most of the time it is the little things that make the biggest difference. Remember to smile. Remember to be kind. Remember to pay attention. Be truthful. Put your phone down. Make people feel important.

Be like Brian today. With his smiling eyes, attentive focus, kind words, and loving heart, he brings joy and connection in a way that leaves you wanting to be better yourself. That is true impact. Follow his lead and leave people better for the encounter.

Father, give me your love and compassion for the people I meet. Help me leave each one better for the encounter.

6

CORE CONVICTION FIVE
DO THE NEXT RIGHT THING

My good friend Rick's comment during a round of golf made me laugh and think at the same time: "I have two players playing out of my bag. One that hits great and one that could use a few more lessons." Rick is one of those guys who can own a room when he walks in. He is tall, confident, and the king of one-liners. Like a walking book of proverbs, he always seems to have the right thing to say. When it comes to golf, however, he is exactly the type of player the game loves: he will do great on one hole and then want to wrap a club around a tree on the next.

In golf, if you shank one into the woods, you have a couple of options. You can cheat and hope nobody sees. You can try to hit a miraculous recovery shot through the trees and make up for it in one big swing, which usually makes things worse. Or, you can chip out, hitting your next best shot.

No, dear brothers and sisters, I have not achieved it, but I focus on this one thing: Forgetting the past and looking forward to what lies ahead.

PHILIPPIANS 3:13

Hitting your next best shot is a great example of my fifth core conviction: do the next right thing. We all make mistakes. It is what you do next that matters. A lot of people will make things worse by trying to cover up their mistakes. Doing the next right thing means *owning* your mistakes and learning from them.

We all have two players playing out of our bag. The goal is as often as possible to keep the club out of the hands of the one who still needs a few more lessons. The best way to do that is to pick your next best shot and then another one and another one. In doing so, you will create momentum in the right direction. Soon, great things will happen.

Father, help me respond to my mistakes with calm and focused intent instead of reacting to them in a way that makes things worse.

7

CORE CONVICTION SIX
MORNINGS MATTER

Several years ago, I decided to build a barn. I had a spot in mind, but I wasn't ready to start the building process. I had to cut down trees, bring in dirt to level the area, and spread and pack rock to provide a firm underlayment. Finally, I had to dig footers and pour a solid foundation.

If I skipped any of these steps, the barn would struggle to stand when a storm hit, and over time, it would collapse. If we believe that preparation is important when building a barn, why do we reject this truth when it comes to ourselves?

My sixth core conviction is mornings matter. It's one of the biggest missing elements in most professionals' lives. How you start your day directly influences how you're going to *win* that day. For me, a great morning routine is essential. It includes feeding my mind, heart, and body before I take care of others.

Plant your seed in the morning and keep busy all afternoon, for you don't know if profit will come from one activity or another—or maybe both.

ECCLESIASTES 11:6

My morning routine begins with reading my Bible and a couple of devotional books. I also write, taking notes about what I am reading and journaling my thoughts. Journaling allows me to process what is going on in my life and take anxious thoughts captive. This frees me up to think about other, more important things.

Next, I pray and meditate. I think a grateful heart is critical. Prayer and meditation help me reset my gratitude every day.

Finally, I exercise. Taking care of myself physically not only makes me healthier, but it also gives me more energy and confidence, which fuels my productivity and enables me to better care for others.

You are worth taking care of first. If you don't, you can't be your best. For me, it is important to do these things before I begin my day. Otherwise, I lack consistency. One more thing—making my morning routine my most important priority means no excuses for missing it. Period.

Don't you want to build your life on solid ground? Prepare your foundation first thing each day. Mornings matter!

Father, grant me the wisdom and the discipline to establish a life-giving morning routine.

8

LOUIE THE PUPPET MASTER

Louie, our golden retriever, has mastered the dark art of manipulation. He knows exactly how to get a treat at any time, day or night. He simply gets our attention to let him out to go to the bathroom, and when he comes in, he gets a treat. He has pretty much conditioned us to do his bidding in this area, like puppets on a string.

On several occasions, I have seen him try to dupe us into giving him a treat by going outside on the porch for a few seconds, looking around, and waltzing back in with the expectation of a reward. I have even seen him fake performance, looking around with his leg briefly up, and then come back in to wait for his treat.

Every now and then, however, he doesn't get his treat. That is when he goes bonkers. He either shuts down and stares at the pantry, does circles around the kitchen, or pants in our faces until he gets past his disappointment.

You want what you don't have, so you scheme and kill to get it. You are jealous of what others have, but you can't get it, so you fight and wage war to take it away

from them. Yet you don't have what you want because you don't ask God for it. And even when you ask, you don't get it because your motives are all wrong—you want only what will give you pleasure.

JAMES 4:2–3

Sometimes, you and I are like Louie. When our expectations are not met, we shut down, freak out in panic, or pout. We have all been conditioned to expect certain outcomes. Those expectations can be especially debilitating or destructive when we place them on other people. Sometimes, we set expectations for others without even telling them.

Often, there is a battle in our minds between what is happening versus what we expected to happen. If we are not careful, our unmet expectations can prompt an irrational, paralyzing, or even destructive response.

I once read that things turn out the best for those who make the best of the way things turn out. Be careful not to get so entrenched with your own expectations that you act like a crazy dog doing circles around the kitchen looking for a treat.

Father, grant me the grace to hold my expectations loosely.

9

A WALK AROUND THE WALL

God had a strange plan for the children of Israel to defeat the walled city of Jericho. I can't imagine what I would have been thinking if my newly appointed leader instructed me, "Okay, here's what I want you to do. Get everyone together in parade formation. A group of you grab this box, put the priests out in front, and give them each a horn. Then, I want you to walk around the walls of the city, carrying the box, blowing the horns, and then come home. Then, do it again tomorrow, and the next day, and the next day, for six days. Oh, and here's the best part, do it seven times on the seventh day, and then just yell as loud as you can!"

I can only imagine what the people of Jericho must have been thinking as they watched the procession on the other side of their formidable wall. They probably paid attention the first day, but by day three or four, they just laughed off those crazy foreigners and went about their business. Then a few days later, there was a thunderous roar, and the walls collapsed. Game over.

To win tomorrow, you must do things today that most people aren't willing to do. Those actions are little seeds that you plant beneath the surface that go unnoticed until they start to sprout. Developing relationships with strategic people who aren't potential customers, calling people just to say hello, writing hand-written notes, serving in the community, or quietly aligning with tomorrow's influencers won't bring you any perceived return today but will create unstoppable momentum in the future when done consistently. The key is setting aside time to work the fields and plant the seeds for next year's harvest rather than just picking today's fruit.

No human wisdom or understanding or plan can stand against the LORD.

PROVERBS 21:30

God will sometimes ask you to do things that don't make sense in the moment. It might be strange and uncomfortable to you, but he is showing you how to compete in a different way. Commit to doing something daily or weekly that prepares you for tomorrow's victory.

Father, show me how to plant seeds today that will yield a harvest of success tomorrow.

10

A RULE WORTH FOLLOWING

Robby, the oldest of three brothers, was a pretty good athlete. In fact, all three boys were special talents on the field. As they each dominated youth sports in their respective age groups, a fair bit of bragging emerged. Much like your friends who tell you about a heroic deed they performed or a huge fish they caught, the boys' boasting started getting out of control.

Their parents didn't like the behavior, so they instituted a family rule that their sons were forbidden to talk about their own accomplishments unless specifically asked about them. The rule didn't stop the boys from achieving great things; it simply stopped them from talking about themselves. It kept them humble.

The Tebow family rule was a lesson that Tim, the youngest of the brothers, never forgot. Even today, the significance of his impact in football goes unnoticed by most because he does things quietly, privately, and behind the scenes to avoid drawing attention to himself. Instead, he gives attention to the One who blessed him with the ability to do great things.

Watch out! Don't do your good deeds publicly, to be admired by others, for you will lose the reward from your Father in heaven.

MATTHEW 6:1

I once read that manmade lights get in the way of God's glory shining in the sky. When we spend too much time shining a light on ourselves, we tend to hide the true beauty of the moment.

The same is true in business. When you seek credit (which we all desire) rather than give credit to others, you dampen the impact of your team and diminish your drive toward future accomplishments. The Bible says to let others praise you, not your own lips (Proverbs 27:2).

Where are you wasting energy seeking credit for a job well done instead of giving credit to others? What acts of service can you quietly perform today, not to be heralded but to be helpful? Who do you know who could use a private act of kindness to brighten their day?

If you continue to do good works, and do them for the right reasons, you will receive your reward. The Tebow Rule is a rule worth following.

Father, fill me with your Spirit so that I might serve others and seek your glory instead of my own.

11

STAY PLUGGED IN

It's incredible how many things don't function properly when the internet is out. In fact, it's quite scary. The Wi-Fi box at our house decided to stop working. While on the surface that might seem like a little inconvenience, all the things it masterfully controls tell a different story. TVs, vacuums, air conditioning units, door locks, computers, and even grills connect to this invisible force. When the internet is disconnected, those things stop functioning properly. Sure, life goes on, but nowhere as efficiently as when the connection is strong.

It is much like us and the Word of God.

Jesus told him, "I am the way, the truth, and the life. No one can come to the Father except through me."

JOHN 14:6

It's amazing how readily we become dependent on Wi-Fi, an invisible source of power and connection we don't understand, yet we neglect the original source of our power and wisdom, the

Word of God. Too often, we behave as if we don't need it or it isn't worth our time.

When we become disconnected from the Word of God, life goes on, but not quite as well as it would if the signal were strong and working in our daily lives. Imagine if you allowed your Wi-Fi connection to work only one day a week. What about for only five minutes in the morning or twenty seconds before a meal? Once or twice a year? I have travelled all over the world to places where people don't have shoes on their feet, a roof over their head, or food to eat, but they have cell phones and Wi-Fi. It is mind-blowing. Can you imagine how our lives, and the world, would change if we valued our connection to God in the same way? He is our primary need before anything else.

Check your connection today. If the light on the connection box thingy is blinking red, or not on at all, you might want to unplug for a minute and reset. Living a life disconnected from God's Word is possible, but it doesn't run smoothly or harmoniously. And it doesn't end well. Stay plugged into your life source.

Father, forgive me for neglecting your Word. It is power for my life. Help me stay connected today.

12

A FIST IN THE AIR AND
A HEAD IN THE SAND

It had been a rocky few months. Since Abraham Lincoln's election just a few months previously, seven states had already seceded from the Union and were working on the formal establishment of the Confederate States of America. Now, on the day of his inauguration, the new president had the nearly impossible job of addressing the country with a message of strength and conviction while remaining careful to embrace the South in a last-ditch effort to avoid a civil war. It was a tough first day on the job!

The following is an excerpt from that speech:

We are not enemies, but friends. We must not be enemies. Though passion may have strained it must not break our bonds of affection. The mystic chords of memory, stretching from every battlefield and patriot grave to every living heart and hearthstone all over this broad land, will yet swell the chorus of the Union, when again touched, as surely they will be, by the better angels of our nature.[1]

It was a brilliant call for reconciliation while simultaneously claiming a future when peace would preside and the Union would survive. A great leader was casting a great vision appealing to all countrymen.

An offended friend is harder to win back than a fortified city. Arguments separate friends like a gate locked with bars.

PROVERBS 18:19

How often do we allow differing opinions to drive a wedge between us instead of practicing harmonious disagreement? Angry offense pushes our families, teams, and communities into our own micro-civil wars. Regardless of how differently we see things, we are not enemies.

Avoid being like the "Angry Young Man" in Billy Joel's song of the same name. He is so stubbornly fixated on his beliefs that he rages against any opposition, but in reality, his myopic view limits his understanding of the world.

Seek to understand, not to be right. When you are *sure* you are right, don't get offended by people who see things differently. Understanding arms you with weapons of compassion, wisdom, and influence. Light a candle of understanding instead of a fuse of offense, and let the better angels of your nature rule the day.

Father, help me seek to understand instead of trying to prove that I am right.

13

A WORD SALAD

When I was in high school, among the yearbook senior superlatives we gave a unique award called "Talks Most, Says Least" to the person who loved to ramble on and on, offering lofty explanations only to end up saying nothing meaningful at all. If the whole world were like my high school, I think a large percentage of adults would see their pictures on that page of the yearbook.

My friend refers to this kind of empty rambling as a word salad. It is throwing so many words and explanations out while trying to deliver a message that you lose the audience. The point might be simple, but it gets jumbled up when we try to sound intelligent or convincing.

There is an art in keeping things simple.

Too much talk leads to sin. Be sensible and keep your mouth shut.

PROVERBS 10:19

You might like the way you sound, but you are not communicating if nobody understands what you are saying. Great communicators take complex things and make them simple. They distill long-winded commentary and boil them down to key, useful points. They focus on winning the award for "Talks Least, Says Most," and as a result, their influence soars. It is not the number of words or lofty speech that matters, it is the *right* words well placed so they are clearly understood.

Whatever you have to say today, don't try to impress. Focus on clarity instead. Here's a hint: the more prepared you are, the fewer words you need. You don't have to fill the space with a word salad, just serve people what they need to hear. Keep it simple, and remember, clarity is kind.

Father, help me keep my communication simple, clear, and kind today.

14

SUPER BOWL GONE WRONG

In 2021, Patrick Mahomes was playing quarterback for the Kansas City Chiefs at such a high level that many people said he was the best player in all of football. Leading what was the best offense the league had seen in years, Mahomes and the Chiefs were not only destined to go to the Super Bowl but were clear favorites to win it. They made it all right, slicing through teams in the playoffs. But when they got to the big game, everything changed.

The Tampa Bay Buccaneers dialed up a defensive game plan that smothered Mahomes. They pressured him on every play, sacked him, knocked down his passes, and chased him all over the field. It was like they had twenty-two players on defense instead of eleven.

No matter what Mahomes did, nothing seemed to work. You could watch his dejection grow throughout the game until his hope for victory faded with the final whistle.

When you go out to fight your enemies and you face horses and chariots and an army greater than your

own, do not be afraid. The LORD your God, who brought you out of the land of Egypt, is with you!

DEUTERONOMY 20:1

Have you ever experienced seasons in which every area of your life feels under attack?

When my life feels like I'm a bad quarterback fighting against a stifling defense, I go back to a few disciplines that help keep me moving down the field. Maybe they can help you too.

1. Start each day with quiet time devoted to reading and exercise.
2. Pray. Ask God for help.
3. Go back to the basics. Focus on a few select tasks *before* you allow attention to drift.
4. Clear out other people's stress and anxiety. It may be too much right now.
5. Remind yourself of important truths. You are deeply loved, and this season is temporary.
6. Forgive. Anger, frustration, and judgment are heavy. Drop them.
7. Go to work. Maintain momentum by pushing forward.
8. Don't battle alone. Ask for help and delegate.
9. Love. Express love to those closest to you.

Don't try to fight every battle at once. Huddle up with those closest to you, bring God in, and run one play at a time.

Father, when I am tired and discouraged, help me get back to basics, trusting you to help me.

15

I WAS A STRANGER

I stepped out of my Uber in New York City, through the cold air, and into the tiny, cramped lobby of my hotel. I was surprised and a little confused when the clerk behind the counter called me by name. That is when my friend and business partner, Henry Santos, came over with a big smile on his face and started talking with the clerks as if they were long-lost friends. I realized that Henry had befriended them earlier and told them I would be arriving shortly.

Later, we walked a few blocks to a restaurant where the maître d' greeted Henry with laughter and a hug before whisking him away to the table. As they reminisced about the last few times he was there, our waiter came by and called Henry by name, and the two had a joyful conversation. After the meal, it seemed the entire staff gathered to see us off.

We went from the restaurant to another venue, and upon entry, Henry greeted the lady behind the counter with a smile, joked a bit, and thanked her. Throughout the evening, he made each person he met feel like the most important person in the room, and they returned the blessing.

Then the King will say to those on his right, "Come, you who are blessed by my Father, inherit the Kingdom prepared for you from the creation of the world. For . . . I was a stranger, and you invited me into your home."

MATTHEW 25:34–35

Later, I called Henry and commented how impressed I was at how kind, attentive, and loving he was to everyone. He responded, "My life is so good, and I am so blessed. I just feel that every person I meet is an opportunity to share my joy."

What a great example of my core conviction of leaving people better for the encounter! It is love in action, seeing people for *who* they are instead of what they can do for you and finding a way to leave them better off.

Notice people. Share a smile. Be interested and grateful. You may be someone's only chance to feel known and cared for today. Don't miss that opportunity. It is an investment that will produce a joyful return of immeasurable results.

Father, may each person I meet today feel seen, valued, and loved.

16

SWEEP THE SHED

Coach K (Mike Krzyzewski) led the Duke University men's basketball team to five national championships over his four-decade tenure. He also coached the US Olympic team to three gold medals. In short, he knew how to put together a winning team.

I once had the opportunity to hear Coach K speak, and I soaked up every word. He said that at the start of every season, he brought his players together and conducted a standards meeting in which he had the team define the standards by which they would operate together. This process ensured a high level of clarity and accountability.

This reminds me of another extraordinary coach, Greg Carvel, who took his UMass hockey team from last place to a national championship over a five-year period. He credited the dramatic turnaround to the culture he and his assistant coaches embedded into the program. They made their focus the character of their players rather than talent.

Coach K pointed out that this sometimes means you have to sweep the shed. Anyone who refuses to meet the standard expectations must go. If you have people on your team who don't buy into the vision and culture, that doesn't make them bad people; it just makes them a bad fit for your team. It is best for everyone if they find a team for which they are a good fit.

One person inside the team who is not on board can derail the entire mission. And one of the fastest ways to derail a mission is gossip and unnecessary drama. Teammates need to have each other's and the coaches' backs.

When a leader listens to malicious gossip, all the workers get infected with evil.

PROVERBS 29:12 (MSG)

Gossiping and drama between teammates must not be tolerated. It's a poison that infects the entire team. The sooner it is removed the better. As leaders, we must have the courage to root out this evil for the benefit of the team and the mission. As teammates, we must recognize that while creating drama or gossiping may draw attention or sensationalize a moment, it will also result in the destruction of the mission or an invitation to join a different team.

Set a vision and expectation for the team's culture; then sweep the shed.

Father, keep my team from harmful gossip.

17

WIDE LEFT!

Heartbreak and *despair*. These are the only words I can think of to describe a kicker's state of mind after he misses a game winning field goal or extra point. Imagine how lonely it must feel to have your team drive down the field, claw their way into position to win the game, look to you to do your one job—squarely placing their hope for pigskin glory on your shoulders alone—*and then blowing it.*

It must be terrible for a kicker who made that kind of error to stand heartbroken and alone among 60,000 screaming fans and players. There is no covering up that kind of mistake!

While most of us don't have to do our jobs in front of thousands of people—or with that much pressure—we are all prone to making mistakes. When we do, it is tempting to try to cover it up, hope nobody notices, and pretend it didn't happen.

The danger of this temptation is behind my core conviction to do the next right thing. When you make a mistake, don't try to hide from it.

Instead, commit to learning from it and getting better. That takes courage and work.

Be strong and courageous, and do the work.

1 CHRONICLES 28:20

In today's Scripture reading, David is speaking to his son Solomon, who was called to build the temple of God. Now that is big-time pressure with nowhere to hide. David knew Solomon would need both courage and strength to get the job done.

The bigger the stage, the bigger the win, and when you mess up, the greater the opportunity to improve. Failure is simply the price you pay for success. Don't be afraid to take the next kick just because you missed the last one. And when someone else misses a kick, be sure to rally around them so they don't bear the weight of failure alone. Help them find the courage to get them back on the field.

You won't score on every attempt when presenting to new partners, talking to prospects, or negotiating deals, but you must keep trying. When you miss, figure out why and hit the practice field. Then get back out there and kick again.

Father, grant me the wisdom to learn from my mistakes and the courage to try again.

18

WORDS AND MUSIC

As a kid, I loved the movie *Eddie and the Cruisers.*

Eddie was the only member of the band who had any interest in bringing in Frank Ridgeway. After all, he was a bit nerdy. His greatest strength, however, was writing song lyrics. It was a skill bandleader Eddie Wilson lacked.

Wordman, as Frank was quickly nicknamed, joined the band, and Eddie and the Cruisers launched into their first album, *Tender Years.* To this day, I still remember a scene when Wilson was talking to his manager about why they needed Wordman, saying simply, "Words and music, Doc. Words and music."

When words and music sync in rhythm, they can communicate powerful messages in a beautiful way. That scene from the movie strikes me as a powerful reminder of how we need to conduct our lives.

Our words and our actions must be in sync, or we risk creating a bunch of noise—or even worse, no sound worth listening to at all.

Beware of false prophets who come disguised as harmless sheep but are really vicious wolves. You can identify them by their fruit, that is, by the way they act.

MATTHEW 7:15–16

We all come across people in our lives who fall into the false prophet category: those who say one thing and do another. These people will blow up relationships and tear apart a team.

It is normal to slip up and say or do something that doesn't line up with your value system from time to time. That is a part of being human, and it is where grace comes in. *Intention* is what matters most.

Overall, a person living a life of integrity will demonstrate consistency in doing the next right thing. Their actions will also match up with their words most of the time. And that is what really matters. People are far more interested in what we do than what we say. Saint Francis of Assisi is widely quoted as saying, "Preach the gospel always. When necessary, use words."

Where are the words and music of your life out of sync today? It may be time for a little fine-tuning.

Father, show me where my actions fail to reflect my words. I want my life to make beautiful music for you.

19

A SCALING LADDER

During the First World War, on the night of March 9, 1918, Colonel Douglas MacArthur joined a brigade of Iowans for a raid against the Germans. MacArthur had been making a name for himself during the war for his eccentric fighting outfit (a letter sweater, tie, and officer's cap). He became known as "the fighting dude" because of his courage under fire, willingness to lead his troops into enemy lines, and what seemed like divine protection from swarming bullets. During this raid, however, the Germans anticipated what was coming and stifled the advancing brigade, pinning the Iowans and MacArthur into the trenches.

According to the book *Team America* by Robert O'Connell[1], this is what happened next:

The Iowans looked up from where they were sheltering in their trenches to see a man wearing a beat-up officer's cap, letter sweater, and necktie instructing their commanders. Not long afterward, "the fighting dude" lived up to his nickname. The courageous general led the way for his troops by scrambling up the scaling ladder first. His men, made brave by his fierce example, followed, and the battle turned their way as a result. For his heroic leadership, MacArthur was awarded the Army's second-highest award for bravery, the Distinguished Service Cross.

As a leader, don't expect your people to do something you aren't willing to do yourself. You are the standard to which your team will rise or fall, so if you want your team to grow, you must grow first. That is tough because it requires that you remain courageous when facing an ever-attacking enemy while possessing the humility to hear input from others about where you need to sharpen your sword.

Trustworthy messengers refresh like snow in summer. They revive the spirit of their employer.

PROVERBS 25:13

Over the years, I have been blessed with a lot of "trustworthy messengers" who are willing to give me input and help me grow. Some feedback I like. Some I don't. Some I disagree with but listen to anyway. Some I wish I had heeded sooner. All of it is beneficial for growth. We cannot elevate others higher than we ourselves have gone. If we want to lift people up, we need to go over the ladder first.

How are you investing in your own growth? Are you leading your team over the scaling ladder into the battle or sending them out to fight the battle for you?

Leadership and life aren't easy, but you were created for this!

Father, give me trustworthy messengers to help me grow and grant me the courage to lead my team well.

20

BLIND BEGGAR

It was 1994. With a degree in my hands and a new growing city around me, I was ready to take on the world.

I secured an entry-level position at a large publicly traded insurance company, knowing that if I could just get my foot in the door, I could find ways to move up. So, I became the expert and committed to being the hardest-working person in the room.

It paid off. I was feeling pretty good about climbing the corporate ladder when I had an experience that hit me in the gut.

Our company brought in a consultant to conduct a review of the senior leadership team, and they asked my team, peers, and supervisors what they thought of me. I produced results, so my boss was happy with me, but everyone else thought I was an arrogant, young jerk.

I was focused more on being right than bringing people in, more on getting the job done than pulling people up.

It was one of the hardest lessons I have learned. The experience helped me see the truth so that I could grow. Before that, I was blind to anything but myself. Now, I pray for eyes that see.

"What do you want me to do for you?" "Lord," he said, "I want to see!"

LUKE 18:41

Here are few lessons from my experience:

1. Being the expert and the hardest-working person in the room is a proven formula for success, but if you don't serve others and leave people better for the encounter, you will soon fall off the corporate ladder —alone.
2. Surround yourself with people who are better than you and equip them to do their jobs. You are only a small part of the best that can be done.
3. If you want to grow your business, grow the people around you. They will do things differently than you, and that is okay. A great leader doesn't need to force their opinion on others.
4. Be sure to look for encounters that help you *see*. Find people who will tell you the truth, and then have the guts to listen and respond to it.

Is it time for you to rethink what success looks like? Pray for eyes that see and ears that hear. God will be faithful.

Father, give me eyes to see and ears that hear the truth.

21

SILENT CAL

Calvin Coolidge was a small-town boy from Vermont who lost his mother when he was twelve, and his sister just a few years later. His father, a hard-working farmer, store owner, and local politician, raised him.

After high school, Coolidge went off to college in Massachusetts and became a lawyer. Soon after, he followed his father into politics. He was known as someone who was determined, quiet, and extremely intelligent. He excelled in debate, public speaking, and writing.

Over the course of his career, he served as a councilman, state representative, lieutenant governor, state senator, governor, vice president, and finally, president of the United States. He battled unions, fought for civil rights, balanced the budget, built roads and infrastructure, cut taxes, and presided over the Roaring Twenties.

Coolidge was introverted by nature. One of the keys to his ability to produce was his practice of taking time away to think. He would often retreat to his room, take long walks alone, and spend time in quiet contemplation. His reserved demeanor earned him the nickname Silent Cal.

It was a leadership rhythm that Jesus embraced, as well.

After sending them home, he went up into the hills by himself to pray. Night fell while he was there alone.

MATTHEW 14:23

Today's Scripture reading recounts one of the times when Jesus slipped away from everyone for some quiet and solitude. He had just astonished a crowd of thousands of people with his teachings before providing each of them with the equivalent of a Happy Meal and a doggie bag. While most of us would celebrate our miraculous accomplishment over dinner and drinks with friends, post selfies, and drop reels, Jesus wanted time alone to prepare for what was next.

In the busyness of life, work, and family, we can't forget to give ourselves time alone to think and pray. Quiet time spent in intentional solitude allows us to rest, refocus, and recharge our minds. Remaining always on with people, screens, and noise, however, eventually fries our brains and empties our hearts.

No one accomplished more in this world than Jesus during his earthly ministry. If the Son of God frequently needed time away for solitude, contemplation, and prayer, don't we? Find a little bit of Silent Cal time today.

Father, sometimes, I need to retreat to advance. Help me prioritize time for prayerful solitude.

22

TIME IN THE COACH'S ROOM

The book of Revelation can take a lot of rereading and deep contemplation to fully grasp, but chapters two and three lay down some straight-up truth. Reading them is like stepping into the film room with Jesus as the position coach.

I know all the things you do. I have seen your love, your faith, your service, and your patient endurance. And I can see your constant improvement in all these things. But I have this complaint against you. You are permitting that woman—that Jezebel who calls herself a prophet—to lead my servants astray.

REVELATION 2:19–20

Like any good coach, Jesus points out the good, the bad, and the ugly, wrapping up each session with encouragement. He enables us to believe that victory will come if we follow the game plan and put in the work. In these addresses to several of the early churches, he lays out things that most of us can claim on some level.

- **Ephesus:** You are patient, steadfast, and don't tolerate evil. Good job! But you're cruising along. There's no fire in your belly. Too much legalism, too little love.
- **Smyrna:** Hold on, stand firm. I know you are suffering, but don't whine about it. It's gonna turn out great. Don't quit.
- **Pergamum:** You have shown great loyalty, thank you. That said, you are tolerating a few bad apples. Clean that up, or the whole team suffers.
- **Thyatira:** I'm impressed by your constant improvement. Keep at it. But you are struggling with temptation. You gotta guard your eyes.
- **Sardis:** Stop chasing public opinion, followers, and likes. Chasing the world is chasing the wind.
- **Philadelphia:** Attaboy! You've stayed disciplined and obedient despite being what the world considers weak. Trust me, I'll take your weakness and make it your greatest strength.
- **Laodicea:** Get off the field if you aren't going to care. Don't just go through the motions. Get in the game, or get out of the way.

Jesus, like a great coach, loves us enough to tell us the truth and encourage us so that we can improve. Get in the film room with Coach and work on your game today. There is some time left on the clock. Use it well.

Father, thank you for telling me the truth and encouraging me to make changes that lead to victory.

23

A COLORFUL REMINDER

After work one Tuesday evening, my wife, Susan, and I decided to walk along the beach to get a little evening exercise, decompress, and share with each other about our day. The sharing part is sometimes more difficult for me. I end up spending much of our time ruminating on several different things and just quietly walking. At one point Susan said, "You are awfully quiet. Is everything okay?"

The question jolted me out of my trance. I began to tell her about the meetings I had that day, what I had been working on, and about my concerns. Sharing with her helped me calm my mind and relax a little. I have discovered that processing my thoughts by talking or journaling is a big part of developing my mental clarity.

After a moment, I looked at the ocean and noticed that the setting sun reflected across the surface of the water turned the ocean a myriad of different colors depending on the angle of its rays and the depth and movement of the water. What a massive and beautiful creation we are given to enjoy!

His glory towers over the earth and heaven! He has made his people strong.

PSALM 148:13–14

My experience on the beach that evening reminded me not to allow the issues I deal with daily to distract me from what is truly beautiful and worthy of my attention in life.

Problems come and problems go. Issues are real and need to be dealt with directly and swiftly. But if we spend all our energy focusing on the hole instead of the doughnut, we will miss the sweetness of life and cherished relationships.

It is easy to get mentally paralyzed by the things we wish were different. Remember, you were made strong enough to handle your problems *and* recognize and enjoy the beauty all around you. When Jesus, the Son, shines on you, an array of beauty reflects out onto the world around you.

Take time to lift your eyes from your problems today to recognize the good all around you. Recognizing and appreciating your blessings will recharge you for your work and energize you to deal with whatever you are facing.

Father, lift my eyes from my challenges and concerns to recognize your abundant and beautiful blessings in my life.

24

BARKING AT THE STOVE

I created a monster. A few years ago, we decided that instead of buying dog food, we would cook more nutritious meals for our aging golden retriever at home to improve his weight, joints, and overall health. His mental health, however, is another story. He is an absolute psychopath when I am boiling chicken and sweet potatoes. His excitement is so intense that he barks and pants. Until he is fed, there is nothing that will get his attention.

That is the way it is with anxiety. Honestly, I am no different than Louie. When I want something or am worried about a situation, nothing can get my attention until that itch is scratched.

Don't worry about anything; instead, pray about everything. Tell God what you need, and thank him for all he has done. Then you will experience God's peace, which exceeds anything we can understand.

PHILIPPIANS 4:6–7

So many areas of life can cause anxiety. For me, most of those moments are when I am not in control or can't predict the outcome of an important situation. I am sure God is amused sometimes at the frequency of my pleas for peace, understanding, and focus. I think about this as it relates to our customers at Churchill Mortgage.

There is so much fear, excitement, and anxiety in the home-buying process that it can derail even the calmest of people. This is especially true of first-time homebuyers. The excitement of buying a home, fear of the cost, and anxiety over whether they will be approved for a mortgage can be overwhelming. This is where my team shines as we ease fears and offer peace to our clients.

The same holds true for your business, as well. Remember that the people you interact with today may be carrying some heavy anxieties under the surface. Until they are fed with information, assurance, and hope, they are barking pretty loudly on the inside.

Maybe you are the one struggling. If so, tell God what you need, and then focus on the ways he has provided for you and delivered you in the past. Standing at the stove barking isn't going to help. He knows what you need and will deliver it at just the right time. He always does.

Father, give me patience and compassion for my clients today. Help me find ways to offer them assurance and peace.

25

WASH IN THE RIVER

As the commander of the Aramean army, Naaman was legendary. He was a strong soldier and a great tactician—revered by his troops, feared by the enemy, and admired by his king. He seemed to have everything going for him until he discovered that he had the dreaded disease leprosy!

Leprosy was a serious illness in Naaman's day. Lepers were typically banished or at least put in quarantine for fear of its spreading. He had to do something quickly. There was a servant girl in his household who suggested that he go to Israel to see the prophet Elisha, whom she knew could heal him. Without any other options, he relented and made the trip to see God's prophet.

When Naaman arrived, Elisha didn't come out to see him. Instead, he sent a messenger with a prescription for Naaman: wash seven times in the Jordan River.

"What?" Naaman replied in anger. "I thought this guy would come out, wave his hand over my skin, and instantly heal me. Instead, he sent me away to wash in the nasty Jordan River? Nonsense!" Naaman stormed away, refusing to do what was asked of him until some of his teammates intervened.

"Sir, if the prophet had told you to do something very difficult, wouldn't you have done it? So you should certainly obey him when he says simply, 'Go and wash and be cured!'" (2 Kings 5:13).

Those who listen to instruction will prosper; those who trust the LORD will be joyful.

PROVERBS 16:20

Naaman finally followed Elisha's instructions and was healed. The commander wanted a magic pill, but what he needed was a dose of obedience.

In business and life, there are no magic pills, overnight successes, or genies in bottles. Nope, it comes down to having the humility to obey the advice of those with more experience and the discipline to do the work.

You can stomp your feet in protest all you want, but you won't get the result without the process. If you want to accomplish something, find someone who has already done it and do what they say, no matter how uncomfortable it may seem. Remember, success is a process, not an event.

Father, I often want the result without the process it takes to get there. Give me an obedient heart.

26

THE CALMNESS OF GENERAL GRANT

I love reading about ordinary people who had an impact on our world far beyond their apparent abilities. Ulyesses S. Grant was one of those people. His story is fascinating. He never wanted to be a soldier, but fate had a different plan. He entered West Point as a young man without means and was surrounded by cadets of far more privilege. He wasn't much of a student either, but his fellow classmates respected him. He didn't shroud himself in fancy talk, clothes, or image, but instead he allowed his character to tell the story of his life.

On the battlefield, he didn't necessarily agree with every mission, but he did his duty. The qualities that set him apart the most, however, were his courage and calmness. When difficulties swarmed around him, he didn't panic. He knew his mission, stayed calm and resolute, and forged ahead.

I found an important lesson in this: It is essential to control your emotions and stay calm in the middle of a storm so that you can think properly and act wisely. Too often I see people fly off the handle when the heat turns up. It seems like they believe louder and faster is better. Some people get so caught up in other people's emotions that they bend from what they know is right and impatiently move in the wrong direction. It is important to slow down, breathe deeply, think clearly, and then act appropriately.

People with understanding control their anger; a hot temper shows great foolishness.

PROVERBS 14:29

Acting in wisdom is not an emotional reaction. It is the fruit of a calm mind and heart. Whether in the boardroom, on the ball field, in the office, or around the dinner table, stay calm, think, and respond. That allows you to honor others, gain perspective, filter through your own convictions, and confidently move in the right direction. Emotionally charged reactions can lead to devastating results.

Father, grant me the wisdom to calm my mind and heart before speaking.

27

RIGHTS VERSUS RESPONSIBILITIES

On January 20, 1961, John F. Kennedy, the nation's thirty-fifth president, stood without his topcoat in the freezing weather on a canvas of deep snow and sunshine to deliver his inauguration address. In the middle of the Cold War, with fears of the nuclear age and deep division within his own borders, JFK wanted to deliver a message of strength, hope, peace, and responsibility.

In his beautiful Massachusetts accent, he spoke the unforgettable words: "And so, my fellow Americans: ask not what your country can do for you—ask what you can do for your country."[1] Yes, Americans have inalienable rights, but we also have inescapable responsibilities.

The one who plants and the one who waters work together with the same purpose. And both will be rewarded for their own hard work. For we are both God's workers. And you are God's field.

1 CORINTHIANS 3:8–9

As the Declaration of Independence states, we have the right to life, liberty, and the pursuit of happiness. I think the key word is *pursuit*. It is our responsibility to *pursue,* or to do the work necessary, to achieve what we want. A joyful, prosperous life does not come from a handout; it comes from a plow and a field. We must plant and water together to receive the reward.

Too often, we focus on our rights (that to which we feel entitled) instead of our responsibilities (the work required to fulfill our desires). Remember, the first thing God gave Adam was a job. Eden was a beautiful garden, but it needed a caretaker, and the caretaker needed a partner. We can't do it alone.

When I focus more on my rights, what I want or feel I deserve, I tend to veer off track and things go poorly. Conversely, when I focus on what I can *do*, who I can do it with, and how I can help others, I receive a much greater return.

Try focusing on your responsibilities instead of your rights, and watch your garden grow in a way that produces an abundant harvest of hope, peace, and unity.

Father, forgive me for focusing too much on all I feel I deserve.
Instead, help me turn my attention to my responsibilities.

28

STAINS

One day, I noticed that the white towel I had next to my sink had small yellow stains on it, as if someone had marked it with a highlighter. A few days after that, as I was making the bed, I noticed the same thing on my pillowcase.

This went on for several weeks. I swapped out the towel and pillowcase for fresh ones, and eventually it happened again. I was starting to worry that I had some strange alien illness until I looked at my hands one morning as I was taking my vitamins. I was holding a few turmeric pills and noticed that my fingers were yellow! Apparently, the turmeric had been rubbing off on my hands without my noticing. It then transferred to everything else I touched.

Sometimes, we don't notice that things are rubbing off on us. Little by little, as we encounter others, we begin to pick up their behaviors, beliefs, and language. Scripture tells us that when Moses met face-to-face with God, the glory of the Lord rubbed off on him to the point that he had to wear a veil over his face to shield the children of Israel from the glow!

When Moses finished speaking with them, he covered his face with a veil. But whenever he went into the Tent of Meeting to speak with the LORD, he would remove the veil until he came out again. Then he would give the people whatever instructions the LORD had given him.

EXODUS 34:33-34

Who are you allowing to rub off on you? If you hang out with toxic people, you will be stained by toxicity. Bitter people will stain you with bitterness. Skeptics will stain you with doubt. Conversely, joyful people will stain you with joy. Encouraging people will stain you with hope, and hardworking people will stain you with results.

If you want the nature and character of God to rub off on you, spend time with him. Start with a few minutes of Scripture reading and prayer each day. Try pausing in a meeting to silently ask for wisdom. Then, you will have the chance to pass on a bit of his glory to others.

Father, shine the light of your glory into my life. Make me more like you.

29

HUNTING OR FARMING?

Oh, the thrill of the hunt!

Hunting is exciting: The preparation, training, and planning. Quietly, patiently tracking prey. Remaining still while waiting, resisting the urge to shift and get comfortable. Blending in with your surroundings. Controlling your breathing until the moment when your prize crosses your path and you take your shot.

Whether hunting buck in hill country of Texas, big game in the wild of Alaska, or the perfect pair of Manolos on the streets of New York, the hunt is intoxicating. You may come home with an unforgettable memory and a prized possession, or you may come home empty handed. What a thrill!

Unfortunately, most people treat building a business like hunting, and they often come home empty-handed.

Those too lazy to plow in the right season will have no food at the harvest.

PROVERBS 20:4

Farming, on the other hand, can be quite boring. You must prepare the soil and plant the seeds, water, pull weeds, and water some more. Farming demands early mornings and late nights. It requires patience, consistency, and persistence. There is little time off since you plant a different crop for each season. It is a never-ending cycle until all that work pays off with an abundant, ever-growing harvest, year after year after year.

A successful business is like farming, not hunting. Sure, you may get a shot at the big one every now and then, but if you want to build a successful career, get busy plowing your fields and planting seeds. Water and care for those relationships consistently over time, and slowly watch them yield an increase that multiplies year after year. It is a process, not an event, and the only way to a predictable, long-lasting, consistent outcome.

Here is what I've noticed: the most successful people in business are the ones who consistently keep farming, even when business is like shooting fish in a barrel. The ones who struggle are those who forget to plow their fields when the hunting is easy. Their lack of attention allows the soil to harden and become overgrown with weeds.

It isn't too late to trade in hunting for farming. Start now and stick with it. It might be hard and boring work, but the harvest is waiting if you just start planting.

Father, give me the focus and discipline to consistently and carefully nurture my business.

30

WHO WANTS A BURGER?

Lynsi Snyder was seventeen, summer break was just around the corner, and she wanted a job. Her favorite burger joint, In-N-Out Burger, had just opened nearby, so she joined the masses waiting in line for two hours to apply. Thankfully, she was hired.

She went to work and learned the ropes slicing onions, chopping tomatoes, and cleaning lettuce. Each day, she showed up and went through the grind of her job without too much attention, earning her pay just like everyone else. Except, she wasn't just like everyone else. She *owned* that In-N-Out location. In fact, she owned all of them!

The only grandchild of In-N-Out Burger founders, Harry and Esther Snyder, Lynsi didn't want to be treated differently than anyone else, so she put herself in her teammates' shoes and learned the business from the ground up. Even though she was the heiress to the business left to her after the tragic passing of her uncle and father, she wasn't above getting her hands dirty. She knew she couldn't ask people to do something she wasn't willing to do herself.

When people work, their wages are not a gift, but something they have earned.

ROMANS 4:4

Lynsi knew she had a gift, but she also knew she had to earn the respect of everyone else, so she got busy working in an unglamorous entry-level position in her own company. Twenty-five years later, she opened the chain's four hundredth store, has a net worth almost as impressive as the taste of an In-N-Out burger, and is the highly respected leader of the organization because she stayed true to herself, understood that caring for the customer starts with caring for her teammates, and did the work.

It has been said that success comes from the mud. You can't expect to be given something you haven't worked to earn. This is true for wages, respect, and friendships. For me, this also applies to my faith. While God's grace, love, and forgiveness are a gift, it still takes daily effort to understand his Word better, accept his guidance, and deepen my relationship with him.

Where in your life can you get your hands dirty today to ensure success in your future? Life is a dirty job, but its wages are worth it.

Father, help me be a good steward in the small things today.

31

THE BEAUTIFUL ART
OF A GREAT PASS

Man, I was special! I was the high scorer on my high school soccer team for several years, a two-time conference all-star, and all-state too! All the pins on my increasingly heavy varsity jacket were pretty impressive until I realized I hadn't developed the skills necessary to succeed at the next level.

Throughout my soccer career, I was a scorer. If you gave me the ball anywhere deep in the opponent's territory, I found a way to put it in the net. That mentality got me some accolades and a shot to play in college.

When I got to campus for summer ball before freshman year, however, the game was different. They played like a choreographed ballet. I played with the grace of a pit bull.

I discovered that scoring is great, but the real hero is the player who makes the pass. I had played my whole career as a headline-seeker who never mastered the beauty of a great pass.

I got so discouraged that I quit.

It's a decision I still regret.

As each part does its own special work, it helps the other parts grow, so that the whole body is healthy and growing and full of love.

EPHESIANS 4:16

If you find yourself frustrated by an ongoing lack of progress in your business, it's most likely due to a lack of great passes. Being a great teammate means doing your job right and prioritizing effective communication. If an outcome isn't great, talk about it with your team and work together to make the next one better. And if you have players who aren't making great passes or are constantly complaining about other teammates, get them off the field. You can't win with them.

I'm grateful for the lessons I learned from not being good enough when I got to the next level. I regret lacking the humility and maturity to recognize it back then and not putting in the work required to improve. But without tough lessons, we don't grow.

When each part does its own special work and helps others grow, the whole team is healthy, growing, and full of love. And love is undefeated.

Father, help me be a great teammate, choosing the good of the team over my own glory.

32

I DID IT AGAIN

We had an old sofa upstairs that was ready for retirement. It was a large sectional, so we called the son of a good friend who had a truck and fourteen-foot trailer for help.

When the young man arrived with a helper, we were thrilled because even after dissembling the couch into five pieces, it was still heavy. Without a doubt, getting it safely downstairs was a two-man job.

After a few trips, I noticed that one last section still needed to go. I figured I could handle it, so I flipped it on its side and drug it to the stairs. As it gracefully slid down the wood steps and onto the wood floor below, I felt pretty proud of myself. Then, I noticed a little resistance. Being the careful person that I am, I did what I usually do: I just pulled it harder. The piece of furniture moved dutifully in response, and as it did, the metal clasp that held the sections together rewarded me with several nice, wide scratches across the dark wood floor.

Beautiful! I couldn't wait for Susan to see what a good job I did.

**Share each other's burdens, and in this way obey the
law of Christ.**

GALATIANS 6:2

So often, my impatience and stubbornness result in serious
unintended consequences. I can get into such a rush to get 'er
done that I make a mess and create more work. Even more often,
my misplaced confidence that I can just do it myself produces
results that are not as good as they would be if I asked for some
help.

Others are blessed when we allow them to help carry the load.
Sharing the work with your team also offers them the opportunity
to learn new skills and grow. Conversely, trying to do everything
yourself creates a lid on your team, and that lid is *you*.

Do you need some help today? Don't hesitate to ask for it.
Doing so will only make you more valuable and your team
stronger.

*Father, forgive me for my stubborn determination to take care of
everything myself. Give me the patience and humility to ask for
help.*

33

AN AFTER-DINNER NAP

The friends had feasted on good wine and delicious bread, enjoyed good conversation, and even sang a few songs together. The stars were out, and the evening was pleasant, so an after-dinner walk on the hillside seemed like a great idea.

Their leader, Jesus, had some big things on his mind and wanted time alone to process them. After asking three of the group to come with him to keep an eye out for bad guys, he went a short distance away to be by himself. Feeling the weight of the world on his shoulders, Jesus dropped to his knees and cried out to God. He was so stressed that he literally sweat drops of blood. His friends, on the other hand, had fallen sound asleep!

Then he returned to the disciples and found them asleep. He said to Peter, "Couldn't you watch with me even one hour? Keep watch and pray, so that you will not give in to temptation. For the spirit is willing, but the body is weak!"

MATTHEW 26:40–41

I used to judge Peter, James, and John for falling asleep when Jesus needed them. Then I realized that on my best days, I can't stay awake during a movie, car ride, or even a football game, not to mention after a great dinner, some wine, and a walk! There have been times when my family needed me, my wife wanted to talk, or the Patriots were winning another Super Bowl, and I was too busy snoring to notice. Additionally, there have been moments when I have been asleep to the needs of people at work or in my community. Sometimes, I am so focused on myself that I fail to see the anguish of others.

We can miss some pretty important things when we aren't paying attention. Even worse are the things we stumble over when we allow our physical desires to rule over our spiritual needs. Jesus needed his friends to be alert, but their physical desires robbed them of the moment.

Good times with great friends are a gift from God, but don't let that cause you to sleep through the moments in life when people need you. Sometimes, your presence is all they need.

Father, help me stay alert for opportunities to ride shotgun during other people's difficult moments.

34

A CLEAN BARN

Do you ever find yourself playing digital *Whac-A-Mole*—getting caught up in all the problems flying at you through email, text, or another form of digital communication?

It is easy to find yourself hammering out responses to the problems that pop up all day long until before you know it, the day has flown by and you are not really sure what you accomplished. Productivity is further diminished because you weren't the only one on the communication string; several people were focused on the same issues, multiplying the collective waste of time. Even worse than that, it is unlikely that the problem on the surface was the most pressing issue. This is called the tyranny of the urgent!

Often, when a problem pops up and we swing our hammer to knock it down, we fail to consider:

- Is it the right problem to solve? The fact that someone else is anxious, angry, or worried doesn't make it your priority.
- Is it my problem to solve? Being added to an email distribution does not mean you are obligated to resolve the issue or even chime in.

- What is the real challenge here? We need to focus on the most important problem instead of the first problem.

Without oxen a stable stays clean, but you need a strong ox for a large harvest.

PROVERBS 14:4

Do you want to have an abundant harvest or a clean barn? When two different challenges are in front of you, which is the most important? If you focus on your short-term anxiety of keeping the barn clean, you may risk the long-term opportunity of an abundant harvest. Yes, you need to clean the stables regularly, or delegate that task, to maintain a healthy working environment for your team, but don't lose sight of our ultimate goal, an abundant harvest. To get there, you need healthy, strong oxen to pull the plow. No ox means a clean barn, but it also means no harvest.

Give up playing digital Whac-A-Mole, and get out of the arcade long enough to think. Only swing at the problems that are your responsibility and are truly worth solving.

Father, give me the wisdom to know which problems to tackle today.

35

A WASTE MANAGEMENT JOYRIDE

I was on a walkabout around the office and struck up a conversation with a teammate named Anthony. He shared with me a heartwarming story about an encounter between his son, Elijah, and the garbage man.

Each week, when the garbage truck enters his neighborhood, the driver, Logan, blows his horn to let Elijah know he has arrived. This is because Elijah loves garbage trucks. As far as he's concerned, there is nothing cooler than the moment when the mechanical arm reaches out to snag a bin off the curb and dump its contents into the back of the truck.

During one visit, Elijah had something very exciting to share with Logan—a toy garbage truck his parents bought for him! It turns out the sanitation worker had a surprise of his own for the child. He gave him a ride around the block in the truck and even provided him with his very own reflective vest and hat that he was allowed to keep. According to Anthony, Logan always goes above and beyond to bring Elijah joy. His reason behind his kindness is simple: "I'm doing God's work," he said.

Anthony feels like Logan's life is a great example of how we each have the power to improve someone else's life. "No matter what your role is," he said, "you can have a profound impact with little effort."

God has given each of you a gift from his great variety of spiritual gifts. Use them well to serve one another.

1 PETER 4:10

What a great example of leaving people better for the encounter!

Life is full of opportunities to engage with others in a way that leaves them better off than you found them. You can offer a smile, a thank-you, a helping hand, or even a ride around the block in a garbage truck. Leaving people better for the encounter begins with *seeing* others, caring enough to notice things about them, and then deploying your God-given gifts in ways that only you can.

Each day is an opportunity to slow down long enough to make someone's day by showing them they are special. How will you leave someone better for their encounter with you today?

Father, help me leave each person I meet better than I found them.

36

WHINERS NOT WELCOME

The Israelites had escaped from more than four hundred years of captivity and were finally standing on the border of the land God promised to them as their new home. They had so much in their favor as they faced the challenge of occupying the land—huge numbers of warriors and a courageous, experienced leader. The scouts they had sent to scope things out returned with a glowing report. The land was indeed very good. It was rich and lush for farming and produced an abundance of succulent fruit. They had waited so long for God's promise to be fulfilled. Now, the time was upon them.

But, instead of jumping up and down in excitement about the opportunity before them, they grumbled in fear. The people were too big, the towns too heavily fortified, the fight too hard. Instead of rejoicing about the possibility before them, they whined about the process to get there. They didn't realize that the struggle would hone their abilities and strengthen their faith. The Israelites didn't want to be uncomfortable, preferring the safety of doing nothing to the glory of change. The result? The Israelites did finally make it into the Promised Land, but not until all those whiners died in the wilderness. Their reward of a promised home had to wait for the next generation.

They said to all the people of Israel, "The land we traveled through and explored is a wonderful land! And if the LORD is pleased with us, he will bring us safely into that land and give it to us. It is a rich land flowing with milk and honey.

NUMBERS 14:7–8

Change is hard. It requires doing things differently, and that is scary. It is uncomfortable, painful at times, and usually full of naysayers. Change takes courage, and, unfortunately, that is a dry well for most teams and organizations.

What potential change in your business holds great promise but you or your team simply refuse to *move*? Why are you afraid? Try shifting your mindset from what you risk losing to what you might achieve. The bigger the opportunity, the harder the work and the bigger the risk, but it is worth it!

Don't surrender the Promised Land to the next generation. Stop whining about what it takes. Go make it happen. Your future depends on it.

Father, give my team the strength and courage to accept life-giving change.

37

A BITTER ORANGE

I was walking around a hotel parking lot while speaking to a friend on the phone when I noticed the orange trees lining the property. They looked great, and I found myself wondering what the rules were about picking one.

Later that day, as I was returning to my room, I passed under another tree. My curiosity got the better of me, and I decided to reach up and snag one. I peeled it, took a bite, and well, one bite was enough. While the fruit looked ready on the outside, it wasn't ripe yet on the inside. What should have been sweet and enjoyable was bitter and nauseating. It was not the right time.

In Greek, the word *kairos* means the perfect time. Sometimes, we have to wait for the right time for either something to happen or to take action, and that is a terribly difficult thing to do.

Until the time came to fulfill his dreams, the Lord tested Joseph's character.

PSALM 105:19

Joseph became not only the man God used to save his people from famine but one of the most influential people in the world. Before he was ready for those roles, however, he endured a lot of hardships to develop his character. He was thrown in a pit and left to die, sold as a slave by his brothers, falsely accused, betrayed, and then stuck in prison for years.

God took his time preparing Joseph. During that long season, Joseph stayed faithful, even though he had no idea what was in store. The period of testing strengthened his character, which was essential before he could be fully used. *Kairos*—the proper time.

Waiting is no fun. Demonstrating the patience required to learn and grow is a true test of our character. Sometimes, we try to force things, only to look back and wish we had waited for the right time. What could have been sweet and enjoyable turned into bitterness instead.

Do you feel you are stuck in the waiting? Is impatience tempting you to force a result? Ask God if it's the proper time for action or if there is something he wants you to learn or character trait he wants you to develop. Don't rush it. God is preparing you for something big.

Father, give me the patience and endurance to wait well.

38

TEMPER TANTRUM AT THE ROCK

I can understand how frustrated Moses must have been. He had spent almost forty years enduring constant complaints as he moved his people from one place to another while trying to teach them a new way of doing things. For decades, every time they were hungry or thirsty, angry with each other, lost or confused, he found a way to scratch that itch. Now, they had reached yet another camp in the wilderness, and once again, there was no water.

> **There was no water for the people to drink at that place, so they rebelled against Moses and Aaron. The people blamed Moses.**
>
> NUMBERS 20:2–3

"Here we go again!" Moses must have thought. So, he went to God for advice. The Lord told him to gather everyone around a specific rock and *speak* to it and water would flow out of it. In my version of the story, Moses thought, "Ah, the old water from the rock trick. We did that one before, but I hit the rock with my staff last time, so I think I'll do that. I know you said speak to the rock, but that's not how we've always done it."

So, instead of speaking to the rock like he was told, Moses struck it. Nothing happened. So, he doubled down and struck the rock a second time. Mercifully, God allowed water to flow out to prove his care and goodness to his people. Moses, however, was chastised for refusing to trust and obey God's instructions. His willfulness caused him to lose his ticket to the Promised Land.

So many of us are like that. We get stuck in our old ways of doing things and refuse to try something new because the old way worked. We ignore the fact that the environment, and therefore the situation, has changed. That attitude puts us at risk of getting left behind.

Progress demands innovation. We must be willing to evolve and challenge ourselves to seek the best that can be done, not the best that we know how. Otherwise, we will be left in the dust while watching others move forward.

Are you being challenged to change? Do it! The Promised Land awaits.

Father, forgive me for my stubbornness. Give me a heart that yields to your will.

39

A NOTCH ABOVE

I *love* competition.

A long-time coworker and I have been in competition for a decade. We will compete over *anything*: Ping-Pong, basketball (I still haven't scored a point here), thumb-wrestling, golf—you name it, we have probably done it. And as much as I hate to admit it, I think he has the edge right now. But not for long!

I love being around others when we are pushing each other to be better. When it comes to certain things like work and exercise, I was wired with batteries included, so I don't require motivation. The competition, encouragement, and shared energy that come along with community, however, helps me step it up a notch above anything I could accomplish alone. I believe *best* is a team effort.

Two people are better off than one, for they can help each other succeed. If one person falls, the other can reach out and help. But someone who falls alone is in real trouble.

ECCLESIASTES 4:9–10

This is one of the reasons I believe that it is better to work in the office together rather than at home alone. Sure, you save some commute time and gas money working from home. Many people feel they stay more focused, as well, but there is no digital replacement for community.

In sports, the locker room is where teams come together. It is where they push each other, share each other's burdens, and hold each other accountable. It is where relationships are strengthened. It is the same with your family, friends, and community.

Another example is the music at church or a concert. Live, it penetrates your heart, and you feed off the energy in the room. Watching the same performance on TV just doesn't have the same effect. That is the power of community.

God gave us his commandments, and he could have left it at that, but he knew that to change the world he needed to *walk with* us not just talk to us. That made all the difference.

Embrace a bit of competition on your team and encourage each other to go a notch above.

Father, thank you for the gift of community. Through healthy competition, help me encourage my team to go a notch above.

40

A NEW FRIEND

I was given a very special gift the other day. Not a fancy watch, book, or new tennis racket, but something much more meaningful: an opportunity to make a new friend. We, along with Louie, our golden retriever, were visiting with friends when their five-year-old nephew, Gray, stopped by.

Louie, who has no use for anyone unless they offer food or affection, naturally assumed Gray was there to give him a dog treat, so he ran over to collect his due from the young stranger. Immediately, Gray had a meltdown. Turns out, he was terrified of dogs.

Throughout the day, I spent time with Gray. I listened to his stories, walked him up and down the stairs just in case there were more dogs waiting to attack, sat with him as he played, and just helped him feel safe. When Louie came sniffing around again, I was able to help Gray through his fear because he trusted me. He had a story in his head about dogs that was real to him, and we needed to create a different story.

After a while Gray relaxed a bit and began to pet Louie a little. The little boy beamed with pride for having the courage to do so. And Louie? Well, once he realized that Gray was just another small human without food, he pretty much left him alone.

Often this is how things play out in our own lives. We fear something either because it is unknown or because we had a past experience that led us to an irrational response. In those cases, it takes someone we trust to help reshape the story so that we can move forward.

I restore the crushed spirit of the humble and revive the courage of those with repentant hearts.

ISAIAH 57:15

If we humble ourselves to realize that we might be wrong and listen to the right friends, especially Jesus, our spirits will be restored and courage can take the place of fear and shame.

Who needs your friendship to reshape the story in their head that is holding them back? Love, listen, and lean in instead of lecturing. This kind of friendship blesses both the giver and the receiver.

Father, give me compassion and understanding for those who are bound by fear.

41

GO NOW

The entire community had been under siege for the last seven years. In fact, over the course of hundreds of years leading up to that moment, they had seen more leadership changes than the New York Jets. Anytime they found themselves on top again, they'd go back to their foolish ways, and someone would sweep in and take them over.

This time around, they were so afraid that many of them were hiding in caves in the mountains and doing their farming and food prep in secret. This was true of Gideon who called *himself* the weakest son from the weakest clan in the whole tribe. He was hiding in a winepress doing his work when God asked him to step up and take a leadership role. Gideon made more excuses than a six-year-old trying to avoid eating lima beans and did his very best to avoid taking action.

I'm not smart enough.
I'm not talented enough.
I'm scared.
Who would follow me?
God told him to stop making excuses and go!

Go with the strength you have, and rescue Israel from the Midianites. I am sending you!

JUDGES 6:14

Too many people waste great talent and ability because they are afraid to fail. There is a need, they have what it takes to fill that need, but they never act. There is always something else that must be done first. Excuses, excuses, excuses. Perfect circumstances are a myth that stagnates progress. The world doesn't need perfection. It needs purpose. It doesn't need excuses. It needs execution.

If you have a purpose and ability, then put them into action. If you see something that needs to be done, do it. Why not you? Go with what you have at your disposal now, and as you are going, more will be given to you to complete the task.

After several more adorable little protests, Gideon reluctantly accepted the call to lead his people, and he was given a great victory. You will be, too. Go now with the strength you have. What are you waiting for?

Father, forgive me for making excuses instead of acting. Help me courageously embrace my calling today.

42

A WOBBLY, OLD, USELESS STRING

I used to own a few guitars. I never actually knew how to play them, but I did enjoy having them sit around the house making me appear musical. Having a guitar is very different from playing guitar. Sure, I learned a chord or two, but I just never made the commitment to learn how to play. Instead, I simply wished an angel would magically bestow the talent upon me without having to go through the process of learning and developing the skill. Unfortunately for me, playing guitar is not magic. It takes work and time.

Once, I broke a few of the strings on a guitar, so I ordered a packet of replacements. Since I didn't know anything about how to string or tune a guitar, the strings just sat there while I waited for my brother to come to town and show me what to do. Guitar strings are useless by themselves. Since they are specifically designed for one purpose, they don't really have much of a function alone. But when they are attached to the head and the body of a guitar, with just the right tension, beautiful music is possible (if in the right hands). One string by itself is capable of a little music, but when all strings are attached together and stretched to each string's optimal place, an endless combination of music is possible.

It is the same with each team, organization, and family. Disconnected and alone, we are not terribly useful. When we come together in harmony, however, it is a different story. In God's hands, beautiful music emerges.

This makes for harmony among the members, so that all the members care for each other.

1 CORINTHIANS 12:25

Coming together in harmony is not always easy. In fact, in my experience, it rarely ever is. It takes time to work together, understand each other's abilities, and learn how to best leverage the collective. Like strings on a guitar, the music comes from tension; not so much tension that a string snaps, but enough to keep in alignment. We each must stretch to achieve harmony.

Don't be a wobbly, old, useless string sitting alone, wishing you were making music. Engage. Attach. Stretch and embrace the tension alongside others. That is where the music happens.

Father, show me how to help my team work together in harmony.

43

A BAD RAP

The dude got a bad rap, forever branded by a single moment of public honesty. He said out loud what so many others were most likely thinking. After all, he had been running with this gang for years, and their leader had just been taken out by their rivals. Then, just a few days later, the word on the street was that he was alive? Of course, his thoughts were a whirlwind of questions and doubts.

Yes, I know he said it would happen. Yes, I know we watched him perform incredible miracles for years. That said, I also watched him get beaten and die on a cross. So, I'm not buying any of this until I see it for myself.

That must have been Doubting Thomas's mindset when his friends told him Jesus was alive, and he had the courage and honesty to say it. Thomas wasn't interested in blind hope. He needed proof so he could then take the necessary action. His questions weren't cowardly; they were bold. The answer he received from Jesus gave him the confidence to open churches all across India until he himself was martyred forty years later.

Do not stifle the Holy Spirit. Do not scoff at prophecies, but test everything that is said. Hold on to what is good.

1 THESSALONIANS 5:19–20

You can't believe everything you read, hear, or think. Sometimes it is in the questioning that you receive the information you need for a bold next step. God's not afraid of your questions, so ask them.

The quality of your answers is directly proportional to the quality of your questions, and the quality of your future depends on the action you take in response to the answers you receive. So, be honest and ask great questions. This is true in your relationships, faith, and work. Be courageous enough to seek the information you need to help you navigate your next step.

Don't fool yourself with ignorance or apathy. Determine to know the truth, even if that discovery gives you a bad rap. Test everything that is said so you can filter out the garbage and hold on to what is good. Be like Courageous Thomas, and once you have the information you seek, act boldly.

Father, I don't want to go along with the crowd. Give me the courage to ask tough questions.

44

BE A STONECUTTER

Most of the mission trips we take involve some sort of construction project and almost always with concrete blocks. Walls, houses, clinics, and wells are all put together with a combination of mortar, concrete, cinderblock, and rebar.

The blocks must overlap in order to lay them properly, which requires cutting many of the pieces in half. Since there is usually no electricity where we work, the tool for this task is the claw side of a hammer or a type of hatchet made for rock. The key is to cut the block straight and clean without demolishing it in the process.

This is truly a less-is-more exercise. The laborer scores the block and then patiently and consistently hits the line repeatedly until the block finally breaks. If he swings too hard, a huge chunk will break off, rendering the block useless. Hitting too softly or getting frustrated and quitting before it breaks renders the laborer useless. If he taps consistently and repeatedly on the right mark with the right pressure, the block will crack in the right spot.

Patient endurance is what you need now.

HEBREWS 10:36

Former Villanova men's basketball coach, Jay Wright, Jr., once said that the stonecutter's credo written by Jacob Riis was part of his team philosophy:

When nothing seems to help, I go and look at the stonecutter hammering away at his rock, perhaps a hundred times without as much of a crack showing in it. Yet at the hundred and first blow, it will split in two, and we know it wasn't that blow that did it, but all that had gone before.

Very little in life is accomplished because of one big swing. Breakthroughs are built one little tap after another. Each team builds upon the effort of the teammates around them. Every generation builds upon those that came before them. Living in such a way that honors those prior generations is so important, lest we leave a crumbled mess of stone for the next.

This is how it is with just about everything—winning championships, getting healthy, building lasting communities, maintaining strong families, saving money, growing business, and breaking rocks. Consistent persistence is the key.

Set your mark, tap tap tap, and don't quit. It is the 101st swing that brings you all that God has promised. Be a stonecutter.

Father, give me a spirit of persistence and consistency.

45

FREE BRAKES

One cold and snowy night, I received a text from one of my closest friends who was on his way to fix his coworker's flat tire. In fact, it was his third tire repair of the day.

Over the last few years, he has offered to perform minor car repairs for his coworkers who, by the very nature of the work they do, put a ton of strain on their vehicles. They don't make a lot of money and often find themselves in a position having to choose between repairing their cars or buying groceries. My friend has offered to remove that choice by fixing their cars for them.

He isn't materially wealthy, but he is one of the richest people I know in the eyes of God.

There are over 49,000 storage facilities in operation today with roughly two billion square feet of storage space available in the United States. We have so much extra stuff in this country that we need an additional two billion square feet of space to store it all!

Is there really that much treasure to store up? I had fallen into that trap years ago and paid to store things I had accumulated that would no longer fit in the attic, garages, or closets. I ended up throwing away ninety-nine percent of it.

Store your treasures in heaven, where moths and rust cannot destroy, and thieves do not break in and steal. Wherever your treasure is, there the desires of your heart will also be.

MATTHEW 6:20-21

I never remember driving over to that storage facility, fumbling with the lock, hurling the door up, gazing inside the storage unit, and feeling my heart fill with joy. On the contrary, I know my friend's heart is full when another single mother who is working hard every day to provide for her struggling family drives away with a free set of new brakes on her car. The last thing he texted me that night was that he has a clarity of purpose. He has a mission, not a job.

Where are you investing your resources? Are your treasures safe in heaven or hoarded away where thieves break in and steal, or moths and rust destroy?

Father, give me a generous heart. Show me how to invest treasures that will last for eternity.

46

PAY CLOSE ATTENTION

Some time ago, I was talking to a business owner who was really struggling. It was a difficult season for businesses in a variety of industries. Many people had more questions than answers. The man to whom I was speaking told me he was asking God to help him get through each day. He said he was focusing on what he could do in the moment and resisting the deception of an imaginary future.

God took the prophet Ezekiel through some wild stuff. God's instructions to his prophet were uncomfortable, outlandish, and at times, borderline vulgar. Ezekiel endured some fantastic and harsh situations as God used him to deliver message after message to Israel and the surrounding nations. God allowed him to go through all of it so that he could teach him important truths that he could pass along to others.

You have been brought here so I can show you many things.

EZEKIEL 40:4

When I find myself in difficult situations, I try to ask myself what I am supposed to be learning that will help me grow. I realize that we are often brought to places that feel dark and uncomfortable in the moment but are orchestrated by God for our learning and growth. It is incredible when I look back on times like those and realize how much better off I am after enduring storms of perfection, as Andy Andrews would call them.

Take a moment to ponder this gem of wisdom from the book of James:

Dear brothers and sisters, when troubles of any kind come your way, consider it an opportunity for great joy. For you know that when your faith is tested, your endurance has a chance to grow.

JAMES 1:2–3

If you are in the middle of a difficult season, be encouraged. This is your opportunity to build strength and endurance and to learn something new! You have been placed in this moment for a purpose. God is showing you many things, so pay close attention. Allow yourself to grow, teach others what you learn, and find joy in the process.

Father, give me patience for the trials I face and help me embrace the chance to learn and grow.

47

A RUN THAT CHANGED EVERYTHING

Years ago, I was in such a heart-wrenching season that I found myself doubting everything I believed about myself and my faith. At the time, I lived at the top of a tall hill. I loved running the road behind my home, which wound steeply down to the valley below. If I timed my run just right, I could catch the sunrise coming over the horizon. The sight always calmed me and opened my heart to God. But not this morning. This morning, I was angry. It didn't take long for me to find myself in a fierce conversation with God about my situation.

"You made me a promise," I angrily prayed, "Where is it?!"

I continued to run and complain, but at the bottom of the hill, the Lord stopped me in my tracks. Deep in my spirit, I sensed his response: "Stop whining! Yes, I made you a promise and it will come true, but it isn't going to look like anything you can imagine. Trust me!"

In his first letter to the Corinthians, Paul quotes the prophet Isaiah, saying, "No eye has seen, no ear has heard, no mind has imagined what God has prepared for those who love him" (2:9).

For since the world began, no ear has heard and no eye has seen a God like you,
who works for those who wait for him!

ISAIAH 64:4

When I began my run that day, I couldn't see that God was actively preparing me for my future. He was equipping me to be the husband I needed to be for the wife he had destined for me. He was also preparing me for the tremendous joy I would experience from learning to trust him. The most important lesson I learned during that time was that joy and contentment aren't a matter of circumstance. They aren't dependent on the love, validation, or opinion of others. Joy comes from knowing that we are worthy of the God's love and friendship no matter what.

If you are in a painful season, remember that the path before you, while difficult, is worth walking. God has amazing things in store for you. Persevere. Listen for his leading. Trust him. He is preparing a more wonderful future for you than you can even imagine.

Father, grant me the grace to trust in you when I am hurting.

48

A CLEAN STREET

Not long ago, I had a healthy conflict with one of our leaders, a discussion I was willing to enter in the first place because I knew I could trust them. I had this confidence because we have put in the work to get to know each other well and have developed a friendship with room to disagree while caring for each other at the same time.

Additionally, we have had several of these discussions over the years, and while I don't enjoy them, I know we have each other's back. We won't attack each other. Instead, we will work through the facts of the issue and wind up at a better place than where we started.

This was affirmed to me when at one point in the discussion my friend made the statement, "We want to make sure our side of the street is clean also."

How can you think of saying to your friend, "Let me help you get rid of that speck in your eye," when you can't see past the log in your own eye? Hypocrite! First get rid of the log in your own eye; then you will

see well enough to deal with the speck in your friend's eye.

MATTHEW 7:4–5

When you work through conflict with people who recognize that there are two sides to every issue and they own one of them, you can truly land in a great place. And you must accept the fact that your side of the street may have a little dirt on it, too. No person or process is perfect.

Without trust, conflicts end in destruction—destruction of teams, solutions, and, unfortunately, people. Conflicts, however, are important. If they are avoided altogether, professional apathy will sometimes destroy an organization's future.

Seek to understand instead of trying to prove that you are right, and stay on the path toward the best outcome. Sure, you will sometimes collide with others, and often with your own ego, but that's necessary. If you are surrounded by people you trust, then you can leave your defenses at home and know that you will be in a better place on the other side of conflict.

And don't forget to make sure that your side of the street is clean before pointing out the dirt across the way.

Father, give me the humility and respect to handle conflict well.

49

HUMILITY MEETS CONFIDENCE

Sergei Kirov was a charismatic and popular leader in his party. He was also a friend of Joseph Stalin, who, back in the early 1930s, had consolidated his power over the Soviet Union and was determined to maintain it. Ever fearful of losing his grip, Stalin saw it as a huge threat to his own power when his friend Kirov won an internal congressional election in 1934. Shortly thereafter, Kirov was dead, along with everyone associated with the plot to take his life.

While the details of who was responsible remain murky, the assassination of Sergei Kirov began what is known as the Great Purge in the Soviet Union, where millions of people accused of being "enemies of the state" were taken out. Stalin was so insecure about his own leadership ability that he removed all opposition. A few decades later, the Soviet Union ceased to exist.

I wrote to the church about this, but Diotrephes, who loves to be the leader, refuses to have anything to do with us . . . Not only does he refuse to welcome the traveling teachers, he also tells others not to help

**them. And when they do help, he puts them out of
the church.**

3 JOHN 9–10

When people are overly concerned with being right or being in control, it saps creativity, undermines loyalty, stifles new ideas, and hinders team growth. This dynamic typically leads to doing things the way they have always been done until the status quo no longer works at all. It is repressive, dictatorial leadership, and I believe it is a recipe for exhaustion and extinction.

Resist the temptation to have all the answers, and instead embrace the process of discovering better answers. Servant leadership means recognizing that the people on your team and others around you may have better ideas better than, or complementary to, your own. Encouraging or accepting those ideas may lead to better outcomes. A servant leader exudes confidence and humility. He encourages better team thinking and loyalty, as well.

Just as trees' roots are strengthened by the wind, it's in the presence of other ideas that our own become better. Humility and confidence strengthen each other when they are allowed to coexist.

*Father, give me the confidence and humility to welcome other
opinions.*

50

BRAD, CHRIS, AND SOUTHERN HOSPITALITY

I could hear a man loudly talking to someone on the phone as I was waiting for my flight. Far from kind, he exuded arrogance with a dash of sarcastic cruelty. He was louder than he needed to be, almost as if he wanted others to notice.

I looked around for a place to sit only to realize that the seat next to him was the only one open. I was tired and irritated after a long day, so I sat down and began thinking about how to shut him up.

That is when I remembered something my friend, Chris Thomas, said about Southern hospitality. He said that embracing the superpower of Southern hospitality makes you feel better about yourself, makes others feel better about themselves, and leads to relationships that thrive.

Most important of all, continue to show deep love for each other, for love covers a multitude of sins. Cheerfully share your home with those who need a meal or a place to stay.

1 PETER 4:8–9

The man finished berating the person on the other end of the phone and looked around for his next victim. I decided to practice a little Southern hospitality by engaging him with kindness and striking up a conversation.

It turns out his name was Brad and he was a Marine veteran from a military family in Ohio and served in Afghanistan. He was single, childless, and traveling alone for a while because he could. He said he believed in being his authentic self and knew he was off-putting to some people. Unsolicited, he guessed my age correctly and then described the act he thought I would have in the circus. At the end of the conversation, he recited two beautiful poems he wrote and proceeded to tell me that he was only ten poems away from his first book. I was glad I met him.

As I boarded the plane, I silently thanked Chris for the lesson in hospitality and thanked God for sending me an angel to practice it on.

Chris defines Southern hospitality as:

- Politeness
- Kindness
- Helpfulness
- Charm
- Generosity
- Intentionality

Our Scripture verse for today takes it all a step further. Hospitality, it turns out, is a Christlike virtue. Try offering someone a bit of Southern hospitality today. It is a great way to leave someone better for the encounter.

Father, give me an open, hospitable, heart.

51

NOT WHAT, BUT WHO

At Churchill Mortgage, we had a meeting with some of our top home loan specialists from across the country not long ago. The purpose of our gathering was to discuss the mortgage and real estate market for the next eighteen to twenty-four months, identify opportunities, and collaborate on different strategies and challenges. In just one meeting, we had a series of discussions engineered to put into practice two concepts:

1. In the multitude of counselors, there is safety.
2. Search for the best that can be done, not the best that we know how.

During one part of the conversation, our teammate Sandi captured the core of what it takes to build a prosperous business and life when she said, "It's not about what you have; it's about who you are."

Sandi is right. If you want to grow your business, be the person people want to be around and trust their business to, and that will be far more influential than any shiny tool, process, or fancy script. I am not saying that these tools, processes, or scripts are unimportant, only that they will simply magnify who you already are. It is the same with money. A jerk with money is just a louder jerk!

A wise person wins friends.

PROVERBS 11:30

As songwriter Jimmy Yeary has said, friends help friends. If you want to grow your business, win more friendships. But here is the catch: to win friends you must first be a friend. Treat other people in a way that engenders trust, empathy, communication, and reliability, especially if you are not yet working with them. In every transaction and interaction with others, there are opportunities to make new friends. You choose who you want to be friends with, so when cultivating business relationships, choose people you want to be around.

I love it when Jesus calls us his friends in John 15:14. What an honor and remarkable connection point for us. Now that's a guy I'd gladly refer business to!

Business is important, but at the end of the day nothing matters more than *who* we are. Follow Jesus's example and love your neighbor as yourself. Friends—and business—will soon follow.

Father, help me be a good friend to others today, following your example in loving my neighbor as myself.

52

BROOM SWEEPING

The garage was dirty, and there was a broom, so I picked it up and swept. To be honest, the whole house was dirty. It made me more than a little frustrated. The homeowner had just moved out and had not been by to clean it yet. It is amazing how much dirt is revealed when a room is emptied and there is nothing left for it to hide behind.

Standing there in somebody else's mess, I had a few choices. I could complain about it, I could walk away and hope the people would be back to clean it in time, or I could do something about it. I chose action. There was a broom in the garage, so I could start making progress. The simple act of sweeping out the garage calmed my anxiety and kickstarted the momentum needed to get the house ready to move in.

The experience reminded me of two important lessons. One of our core foundations at Churchill Mortgage is to be a broom sweeper. Whoever is closest to the broom sweeps. It doesn't matter what your job title is, if there is something that needs done and you are capable, then do it. Also, make sure that you do your job in such a way that it doesn't leave crumbs for other people to clean up, and then go help others get their jobs done, as well.

Being a broom sweeper multiplies productivity, generates momentum, and enhances your team.

For everything that is hidden will eventually be brought into the open, and every secret will be brought to light.

MARK 4:22

The second lesson is that all the dirt that was hiding behind the furniture is a good example of how most of us live our lives. We think we can hide the things we don't want others to see. Ultimately, that is impossible. Most of us need to spend more time cleaning up the corners and behind things, or the dirt will build up and life will become messy. We all have issues. Don't hide them. Claim them, learn from them, turn from them, and prosper.

Being a broom sweeper is an important concept in life. It applies to your team, business, family, and especially your own mind. Sweep up around your habits and behaviors consistently if you want to avoid a big mess later.

Father, help me be a broom sweeper today.

53

ANOTHER LESSON FROM KING LOUIE

You could set your watch by his schedule. At the same time every morning, King Louie (our elderly golden retriever) takes me for a walk outside to take care of business. As he is directing me to our destination, his attitude is directly connected to my ability to stay present. My ability to stay present, however, is directly correlated to my phone.

When I leave my phone in the house, Louie is excited and has some pep in his step and a smile on his face. When I am walking and checking email or sending text messages, he drops his head, walks slower, and pouts.

It's a striking reminder of how staying present makes all the difference.

The algorithm of influence says you must first connect with the heart, then challenge or inspire the mind, and that leads to influencing others. You can't connect with the heart if you aren't present to do so.

Then the people of Israel were convinced that the LORD had sent Moses and Aaron. When they heard

**that the LORD was concerned about them and had
seen their misery, they bowed down and worshiped.**

EXODUS 4:31

One of my personal struggles continues to be the screen of
distraction. I feel a constant temptation to check emails, respond
to text messages, and answer phone calls, even when in meetings
and conversations with others. When I allow that temptation to
win, I lose my ability to connect. If I don't connect, I don't influence and I can't lead. Not even my dog.

Before anyone will follow you, they must believe you care
about them, and caring begins with presence. This is especially
true with your family. When the Israelites realized God was
concerned about them and *saw* them, they followed him.

Stay present. Connect with the heart. Earn the right to challenge and inspire the mind, and then gain influence with others.
And when walking your dog, leave the phone inside. They want
your attention, too.

*Father, sometimes I struggle to stay present for the people who are
most important to me. Help me resist distractions so that they may
know I see them and care for them.*

BRING IT ABOUT

Have you ever wondered why two people with similar skill sets and the same amount of time in the day can have vastly different outputs?

Bum Phillips, Coach Bear Bryant's assistant coach at Texas A&M, had this to say about the legendary coach's leadership ability: "Bryant can take his'n and beat your'n, and then he can turn around and take your'n and beat his'n."[1] For those of you not fluent in Southern drawl, that means that no matter which team Bryant was playing with, he was going to win. Why? He believed he could!

For I can do everything through Christ, who gives me strength.

PHILIPPIANS 4:13

Success comes from a combination of believing that a better result is possible and taking responsibility to bring it about. From there, add a willingness to do the focused work it will take to reach the goal and be consistent with that effort over time.

Did you know that most athletes only push themselves to forty percent of their ability? They stop trying when they get to the point when their body starts to send their mind signals that they are at their max output. The problem is that's a lie. So, they give up and watch the truly elite—who believe they *can* and have owned the responsibility to make it happen—run right past them.

Parkinson's Law states, "Work expands so as to fill the time available for its completion." This means that most people will use all the time they mentally allow themselves to complete a task. It isn't that the task requires that amount of time, but that we make up a fictional time allotment in our minds and then make it true.

What if you picked one result to double today without giving yourself more time to accomplish it? After you check that off your list, pick another result every few days. Continue on that path until you discover the incredible momentum you have created simply by choosing a different way of thinking. The best that can be done begins with believing in a new possibility and then owning the responsibility for bringing it about.

Father, give me a vision for what is possible and the discipline to see it through.

55

A FOUNTAIN NOT A DRAIN

I will never forget a call I received from a respected friend and teammate. He is one of the finest talents in the mortgage industry. He not only has tremendous mortgage and real estate knowledge, but he is also gifted in the economics of the business. In other words, he is super smart.

But none of that had anything to do with his call. Instead, he wanted to share with me about the volunteer work he and his team engaged in the day before and discuss how they could do more. The energy in his voice was inspiring.

He and his team served at Grace's Table, an organization that operates programs and housing for teen moms who otherwise have no place to turn. They provided much-needed repairs and maintenance to the facility, landscaped the grounds, and built a playground. They were a blessing, and in return they were greatly blessed. Our call reminded me of an important truth: the real path to prosperity starts with loving others and giving generously.

But while knowledge makes us feel important, it is love that strengthens the church. Anyone who claims to know all the answers doesn't really know very

much. But the person who loves God is the one whom God recognizes.

1 CORINTHIANS 8:1–3

Talent, intelligence, and knowledge are critical in this world. God blesses everyone with unique measures of each. These gifts should be cultivated, honed, and utilized professionally. That's what it means to be a good steward of the resources we have been given. But these gifts are not what strengthens families, teams, and communities. Only love can do that, pouring out our resources for others from the abundance we have been given.

I'm always amazed that the more people give, the more they are able to do so. In other words, love and generosity are a fountain that doesn't run dry. A drain, on the other hand, collects everything it can and never gives it back.

We all know both types of people: fountains and drains. There are those who always seem to help, energize, and lift you. Others, while intelligent, suck the energy out of the room and leave you exhausted and checking your wallet.

Which will *you* be today? A fountain or a drain?

Father, fill me with your Spirit today so that I might be someone who loves, gives, and serves generously.

56

A LESSON IN GRACE
FROM COACH PRIME

If you watch college football, you know that playing both sides of the ball is uncommon and demands a unique athlete. It not only requires two different skill sets, but also different mindsets, as well. It is also physically difficult, since playing both offense and defense prohibits the player from getting as much rest as everyone else. He truly needs to be a superior athlete.

Travis Hunter, who played for the University of Colorado and in the NFL, is one of these elite talents. He not only plays both offense and defense, but he is also one of the best at both. That is why it was such a shock when he took a devastating hit early in the game against rival Colorado State and was sent to the hospital.

The optics indicated that it was a dirty hit. There were even death threats against the CSU player and his family. I am sure both Hunter and his coach, Deion Sanders, were angry. After all, the superstar was significantly injured and out of commission for weeks.

> **Do not seek revenge or bear a grudge against anyone among your people, but love your neighbor as yourself. I am the LORD.**
>
> LEVITICUS 19:18 (NIV)

An article quoting both Coach Prime and Travis Hunter offered their impressive response to the incident.

Travis Hunter: It's football at the end of the day, that stuff happens.[1]

Coach Sanders: [He] is a good player who played a phenomenal game. He made a tremendous hit on Travis on the sideline . . . This is still a young man who is trying to make it in life . . . He does not deserve a death threat over a game.

Grace. Hunter and Sanders could have blasted the kid and his coach and demonized the play. The whole world saw it and wouldn't blame them if they did. Instead, they led with grace. Both men seemed to understand that they had to let the incident go to move forward in a healthy way. The heavy weight of a grudge would only hinder them.

One doesn't carry a grudge but drags it behind like an anchor. Sure, sometimes people do you dirty, and it hurts, but if you want to succeed, you have to lead with grace. Which anchors of resentment are holding you back? Release them so that you can run into your victorious future.

Father, help me rise above animosity and respond with grace.

57

PROVERBS DEFINITION
OF A TEAMMATE

During the normal ebb and flow of our business, we inevitably have seasons in which revenue slows. When that happens, we have a responsibility to align our team around the realities of the business. It is no fun, but it is necessary, and when that occurs, it is important to have well-defined standards about the kind of teammates we want working alongside us.

In one season like this, I came across the following verses in the book of Proverbs. It struck me how consistent they were with Patrick Lencioni's definition of the "Ideal Team Player." According to Lencioni, an ideal team player is someone who is hungry, humble, and smart. [1]

Kind words are like honey—sweet to the soul and healthy for the body.

There is a path before each person that seems right, but it ends in death. It is good for workers to have an appetite; an empty stomach drives them on.

PROVERBS 16:24–26

At Churchill Mortgage, we have expanded on Lencioni's concept a bit, and it looks like this:

- **Hungry:** "It is good for workers to have an appetite." We want people on our team who are still hungry to produce, make a difference in the lives of others, and show up every day (on time) and work hard. We can't do this for them. They must be self-motivated.
- **Humble:** "Kind words are like honey," and "There is a path before each person that seems right, but it ends in death." We need teammates who are constantly in search of the best that can be done, not the best that they know how. These are people who realize they aren't always right and are committed to treating others with kindness.
- **Smart:** *"From a wise mind comes wise speech."* Ideal teammates are committed to being the expert. They continuously pursue wisdom so that they can put that wisdom into practice. They are people who are smart in their dealings with other people and evolve to meet the needs of the market.

Hungry, humble, and smart. If God calls us to those standards, don't you think they are probably pretty good values for our businesses and families as well?

Father, help me be a teammate who is hungry, humble, and smart, and empower me to develop those same characteristics in my team.

58

SEVEN STRAIGHT

As the Jacksonville Jaguars headed into November with one of the worst records in the league at two wins and six losses, there didn't seem to be much hope of the team making the play-offs. Since their second-year quarterback was struggling to find his groove and their rival, the Tennessee Titans, held a commanding lead in the division with only one loss, nobody gave them much of a chance. Except, of course, the Jaguars themselves.

They believed in their plan and each other and went to work. Day after day, they focused on grinding out incremental improvements while never losing sight of what was possible. It paid off. They won seven of their last nine games and defeated the Titans to win the division. The Titans, on the other hand, lost their last seven games, and earned the bitter reward of watching the Jags in the playoffs.

Finishing is better than starting. Patience is better than pride.

ECCLESIASTES 7:8

A football season is looooong. It's tough to stay healthy, focused, and energized over such an extended time. For players, the grind is relentless. If that weren't tough enough, they also have to juggle the distractions of family, news media, and life in general. Sure, getting started is exciting. In the beginning, everyone is filled with anticipation of what is to come, ready to execute the plans they have been working on for months, and fired up about the prospects of what is possible. Then, they start getting hit, and everything changes. That is why only a few teams make it to the playoffs.

It is also why so many projects, businesses, marriages, and relationships fail. It is hard. If any one person loses their focus, patience, or passion, the chances of long-term success go down significantly.

Stay focused on your purpose, and understand what you are working toward. Seek clarity if you need it, and offer clarity if you have it. Show up every day, do what is necessary to advance, and be patient. When you get hit, get up, trust your teammates, and recommit. Don't let temptations and distractions take your eyes off what is most important. The season isn't over. You can still come out on top, but you can't rest on yesterday's victories. You have to get out and compete today.

Father, give me the focus, patience, and passion to finish well.

59

AROUND THE KITCHEN TABLE

Years ago, my mentor and Churchill Mortgage founder, Mike Hardwick, gave me a book written by his aunt, Mary Clement, titled, *Around the Kitchen Table: Lessons Learned and Lives Shaped.*

In the book, she recounts stories, lessons, and connections that were made simply because people took the time to be present with each other over meals and engage in meaningful conversations.

While the concept is simple to understand, it is difficult to pull off these days. Schedules don't line up. Screens distract us. People don't want to be vulnerable or engage (especially the sub-human species commonly known as teenagers). And, well, we are tired.

At home and in business there is nothing like sharing a meal with others to build connection and relationship.

And these words which I command you today shall be in your heart. You shall teach them diligently to your children, and shall talk of them when you sit in your

house, when you walk by the way, when you lie down, and when you rise up.

DEUTERONOMY 6:6–7 (NKJV)

One of the dinner rituals Susan and I have adopted in our home is a conversation we call "High, Low, Funny." During the meal, everyone takes their turn talking about the high and low points of their day and something that made them laugh. We do it at just about every meal and nobody gets a pass, first-time guests or not. We have found that simple approach to be the kindling that lights the fire of meaningful communication while providing a safe place for vulnerability and laughter.

In all the craziness of your life, take time to get around your kitchen table. It won't happen by accident. You need a plan to be present and communicate. We all crave connection and a safe place to be vulnerable. We don't know what each other is going through, so put in the effort to find out. Teach the life-changing lessons you want to implant in your family's hearts and minds.

What made you happy today? What made you sad? What made you laugh? Remember, the first step in influencing others is to connect with the heart, and then you can inspire and challenge the mind and gain influence.

Father, remind me to prioritize sharing a meal to build connection
and relationship with the people in my life.

60

BATTERIES AND FROGS

I'd like to find and strangle the person who invented the chirp that comes from the smoke detector when the battery dies. On second thought, they should probably be given a Nobel Prize for effectiveness (if such a prize even exists), as there is unlikely a more effective system to motivate a particular action. That chirp is the universal signal to get up in the middle of the night, try to find a nine-volt battery (who has those lying around?) and a ladder and change the stupid battery.

The smoke alarm chirp of death reminds me of Brian Tracy's book *Eat That Frog*. The premise of the book is that we should take care of the most important tasks of the day first, even if it is something we are dreading. Ordinary people who are great at setting the right priorities each day are far more effective than geniuses who don't.

Mark Twain once said that if the first thing you do each morning is to eat a live frog, you can go through the day knowing that is probably the worst thing that is going to happen to you. When it comes to your priorities, the frog is typically the thing that will just get more distracting if not dealt with.

For if a man cannot manage his own household, how can he take care of God's church?

1 TIMOTHY 3:5

Too often we forget to take care of what is most important, because we just don't like doing it. No matter what your to-do list looks like, remember that your most important responsibility each day is *you*. Your health and your relationship with God, your spouse, and your family. If those priorities are not in order, you won't be as effective with everything else.

What have you been putting off because you are dreading it? Maybe it is a phone call to a difficult client, looking over your budget, or telling someone you are sorry. We all have important and unpleasant tasks that we need to address, and procrastinating only makes things worse.

What frogs are you facing today?

Father, give me the discipline to take care of the tasks that I am dreading.

61

THE OTHER BROTHER

Growing up, my best friend's middle name was Jude. We became friends in first grade and remain so today. In fact, he is much more than a friend. He is my other brother.

One day, when I was still just a kid, I stumbled across the song "Hey, Jude" on the B-side of a Beatles album while spinning through my mother's vinyl records. It is no surprise that I was immediately hooked. After all, it was my best buddy's name! Even today, I still can't get the "take a sad song and make it better" line out of my head.

Many years later, when I accidentally tripped over a Bible and started flipping through the pages, I saw that Jude wrote a book! (Actually, a letter that they call a book in Bible talk.) It was short, so I could read it without too much distraction. I discovered that Jude was the brother of James, who was the brother of Jesus so that made Jude the other brother, like my friend Randy!

Just like Randy has done for me many times over the years, Jude was writing to his friends to warn them against allowing their personal desires and deceiving influences to drive their behaviors.

These people are grumblers and complainers, living only to satisfy their desires. They brag loudly about themselves, and they flatter others to get what they want.

JUDE 16

Belief systems matter, and it is important to keep our motives pure, not deceptive or self-serving. People who are grumblers, complainers, and chase their own desires at any cost will ultimately wind up at the wrong end of the battle one day. Refuse to follow their example, and check yourself to make sure you aren't one of them. Throughout my life, I've needed friends to challenge me to stay on the right side of that ledger. As Ben Franklin once said that a man wrapped up in himself makes a very small bundle.

Who is your other brother who tells you difficult truths without judgment? Who has the authority in your life to flip you on your B-side when the primary track isn't sounding so good? If you don't already have that person in your life, find someone and let them in. While you are at it, trip over the Book and let *him* in.

Father, send people into my life who love me enough to check my motivations and my pride.

62

EIGHTY-EIGHT STRAIGHT WINS

John Wooden, the UCLA men's basketball coach from 1948 to 1975, has always been one of my favorite coaches to study. During a twelve-year period, he won ten national championships and at one point, had an eighty-eight-game winning streak. He was a brilliant strategist who knew the game, and his results proved it. More than that, he equipped his players to lead lives of integrity and influence after basketball. He was a coach in the true sense of the word.

Almost twenty years ago, I took notes on a few principles he taught:

1. Be true to yourself.
2. Help others.
3. Make each day your masterpiece.
4. Drink deeply from good books, especially the Good Book.
5. Make friendship a fine art.
6. Build a shelter for a rainy day.
7. Pray for guidance and give thanks for your blessings each day.

Remembering that note prompted me to do a little reading on Coach Wooden, and I ran across a few more lessons he taught. One statement he made really struck me: "Remove all excuses for getting to the next level. Don't say 'No.' Ask 'How?'"

The best requires going far deeper than our current understanding. That includes the processes you develop, the people you choose to be part of your team, and the techniques you use to achieve your goals. It even extends to the technology you use and the products you offer. Going deeper requires a commitment to our core conviction of being the expert, and if you want to be the expert, you need someone who loves you enough to draw out your best.

Though good advice lies deep within the heart, a person with understanding will draw it out.

PROVERBS 20:5

Everybody needs a coach. Who is helping you see what you can't see on your own? Who is helping you do one more rep when you think you are spent? Who is helping you understand more deeply the things you thought you knew? Who is driving you to get better every day?

Don't be content with your current results. Find a coach who will help you remove excuses, go deeper, and continue to make progress towards what is possible.

Father, lead me to the coach I need to help me be the best that I can be.

63

THE MOST IMPORTANT GIFT

"I feel alone in a crowded room."

I have heard that statement countless times. Sadly, we have all been there. Either the crowd makes you uncomfortable, or you feel inadequate around others who seem to have it all together. Maybe you think you have nothing to contribute to a conversation, or maybe the baggage you are carrying is simply too heavy to allow you to engage with others. So, you wander around, void of any connection, feeling unnoticed, anxious, or sad.

How does that apply to your daily life? Many of us go through the motions, wondering if anybody really knows or cares about us. People have always felt this way, but even more so now as we are exposed to the artificially enhanced versions of others through the filters of social media.

You were cleansed from your sins when you obeyed the truth, so now you must show sincere love to each other as brothers and sisters. Love each other deeply with all your heart.

1 PETER 1:22

I once heard mental health expert John Delony say that the greatest gift you can give somebody is to see them and let them know that you love them. I have failed to do that countless times.

How often do I fail to *see* my family, children, teammates, or spouse? Make a true connection? It is easy to get so consumed with ourselves that we forget to even see others.

Everyone around us is carrying some sort of baggage underneath the surface. It is our primary job to stop long enough to see them, recognize that they are important, and offer them love. Love is a verb! It is an act of kindness, empathy, care, and connection, and it all starts with ensuring that people know you see them.

Pay attention to those around you today, starting with your own household. Slow down long enough to find out what they are going through and make sure they know they are loved. Connect with your clients, partners, and teammates in the same way. Leave people better for the encounter by making sure that no one feels alone in a crowded room.

Father, help me slow down enough to see and value the people who cross my path today.

64

HOME REPAIR

When we were having a little bit of work done on our home (nothing major, just surface stuff mainly), things didn't go exactly as planned, but for the most part, we were happy with the result. In the process, we had two very contrasting experiences between the flooring contractor and the woman hanging our wallpaper.

The wallpaper took forever! She started on time, but the work was tedious, and she was committed to doing it correctly. There were many times I wished she was finished. When I walked into the completed rooms, however, I was delighted with the end result. Whenever we need wallpaper hung in the future, she will be the person we use because we know we can trust her to do it right.

Now, the floors were an entirely different story. Those guys started a week later than they were supposed to but committed to being done on time. They came in like a hurricane, cranked out the job in no time, and got out. The only problem was that they left a total mess in their wake. They completely forgot a closet, which meant they had to rush back in again and irritate us a second time. They were so focused on just getting the job done that they paid no attention to details or our experience. Their sloppiness and inattention lost them a customer along the way.

One person cared only about getting the job done fast, whereas the other focused on ensuring that her work delighted the customer.

Work willingly at whatever you do, as though you were working for the Lord rather than for people.

COLOSSIANS 3:23

Sure, people want the job done fast and with enthusiasm but also with a high level of quality. Be clear about the expectations up front. Don't convince people to work with you just because you can get something done fast. Your job is to get it done right and on time.

Don't leave a trail of unintended consequences behind you for others to clean up. Work as if you are working for the Lord. Take the time to do things right and with enthusiasm. People will forget how fast you did your last job, but they will always remember how well you did it and how you made them feel in the process.

Father, help me work with excellence and intention today, as if I were working for you.

65

THE SUN AND THE MOON

You've been there, in one of those moments that simply couldn't be captured with a camera. You see an image so vast, deep, and beautiful that you try to capture in a photo so that you can share it with others. The problem is that when you look at the photo, it falls painfully short of the real thing.

I was out on a walk and feeling a little anxious about all the things I had on my plate. I was tired, not feeling my best, and just trying to prepare for the day. Then I noticed that if I looked in just the right direction, I could see the sunrise out of the bottom corner of my left eye, and out of the top corner of my right eye I could see the moon. It was a fascinating image. They were both in view and shining brightly. It made me appreciate the enormity of the world and realize just how small my worries were.

It also reminded me of how beautiful life can be when two totally different things coexist without comparison or jealousy. Too often we get so caught up in our differences that we create division where there could be harmony. We focus on what someone else has or can do instead of joyfully bringing forth the perfect talent embedded uniquely in us. Spending our time comparing ourselves to others creates fear and anxiety, which diminish our ability to bring value to the world. It also causes relationships to crumble.

A peaceful heart leads to a healthy body; jealousy is like cancer in the bones.

PROVERBS 14:30

Pay careful attention to your own work, and reap the satisfaction of a job well done. The sun can't be the moon, and the moon can't be the sun. Both have vastly different purposes and are needed. Let your own light shine. Don't hide it behind the clouds of comparison and jealousy. Instead, go and do good work with the abilities you have, and accomplish what you have been called to do.

Father, keep my eyes on my own calling. Protect my heart and mind from jealousy.

66

CHOOSE YOUR FLAVOR

Discipline: it is either self-inflicted or self-imposed, reactive or proactive. It is self-inflicted when our behaviors or actions require correction from an outside force, either a person or an undesirable result. It is self-imposed when we proactively recognize, usually through past correction or undesirable results, the right behaviors or actions necessary to accomplish a desired outcome and commit to that on our own. Either way, a life of discipline is unavoidable, but you do get to choose the flavor.

No discipline is enjoyable while it is happening—it's painful! But afterward there will be a peaceful harvest of right living for those who are trained in this way.

HEBREWS 12:11

Jocko Willink writes that discipline equals freedom. This means that the more disciplined structures we commit to in life, the more consistent our results will be, and the more freedom we will have to make choices on all the things we want to do. Today's Scripture reading tells us that discipline leads to a peaceful harvest that will not only lift us up but strengthen others, as well.

Stop allowing yourself to be trained by the consequences of an undisciplined life. Running your business according to whichever way the wind blows will ultimately yield an inconsistent and undesirable result. The same is true about everything else—your health, marriage, family, and finances.

Choose what is most important to you. Build structure around the activities that lead to the desired outcomes. Have the discipline to commit with consistency to those activities, without excuse or exception. This will lead to a life of peace, an abundant harvest, and the freedom to discover all that God created you to be.

Today, pick one area that you want to shift from the reactive discipline of consequences to the proactive discipline of creating results. A peaceful life is waiting for you.

Father, fill me with your Holy Spirit so that I might live a
disciplined life for your glory.

67

MULTIPLY YOUR LIGHT

King David was tired. Why wouldn't he be? He had been in and out of power for years and had suffered his share of challenges. He started his military career in a public, one-on-one fight against a giant, and at the time of today's Scripture reading many years later, he was facing an army of giants again. He was weak and exhausted.

With too few resources to face the battle before him, he found himself backed into a corner. His men rescued him, but not without offering him a loving rebuke. They basically said, "Listen, old man, you are a great king, but you have become a liability on the battlefield. No mas."

And when David and his men were in the thick of battle, David became weak and exhausted. Ishbi-benob was a descendant of the giants; his bronze spearhead weighed more than seven pounds, and he was armed with a new sword. He had cornered David and was about to kill him. But Abishai, son of Zeruiah, came to David's rescue and killed the Philistine. Then David's men declared, "You are not going

out to battle with us again! Why risk snuffing out the light of Israel?"

2 SAMUEL 21:15–17

One of the hardest things to do as a leader is to let go and transfer responsibility and authority to someone else. Most of us feel that nobody can do things the way *we* can. Others fear becoming insignificant or unneeded. *We don't want to lose control.*

While delegating authority and responsibility is one of the most difficult things we will ever do, it is also one of the most powerful. It offers us the opportunity to train others to own their results, execute, and lead. It's not giving up control or responsibility; it's transferring and expanding it.

If you can't trust your team to take ownership of their results, you will wind up exhausted. At some point, life will catch up with you, and if you haven't transferred the fire inside you to someone else, your light may be snuffed out. If you do it well, however, and fight alongside them for a while, you will discover that they will have your back, drag you out of the way, and take the reins at just the right time.

Father, loosen my grip on the reins of control. Help me delegate responsibility to those I am leading.

68

GONE FISHING

Growing up, I remember going ice fishing with my dad a few times. We drove out to the frozen lake, walked out to what we thought was the right spot, dug a hole in the ice with a hand-operated auger, baited the hook, and dropped a line in the frigid water. Finally, freezing cold, wet from digging holes, and impatient, we sat down to wait. I loved spending time with my dad, but the rest was pure torture.

That is why it surprised me when I found myself fishing in the middle of winter again. This time, however, my kids and I were fly-fishing in a river rather than ice-fishing on a lake. There was something magical about standing in the icy waters with the sun beating down, casting and watching as the indicator floated by, tempting the fish below.

I learned a valuable lesson at the end of the day. My son, Ethan, had snagged a few fish but my daughter, Ella, hadn't had any luck. She had several bites, even pulled a few fish up from the bottom, but they kept getting away. And me? Well, the fish had a blast laughing at the old fool standing in the water throwing string back and forth, pulling up weeds, and tangling his line.

As the time to leave approached, the sun started going down, and the cold settled in, but Ella had zeroed in on a spot where a fish kept biting. She wasn't giving up. One more cast, then another, then another. She wasn't going to quit. The fish was there, and she was gonna catch it. Finally, after patiently dropping the line into to same spot repeatedly, she did. And it was a beautiful fish!

So let's not get tired of doing what is good. At just the right time we will reap a harvest of blessing if we don't give up.

GALATIANS 6:9

Success is a grind. It's trying once more after everyone else has quit. One more phone call, one more lead, one more thank-you note, one more hour. It's repeatedly doing the right activities until the desired result emerges.

Perseverance and patience are the key. Keep tossing your line out today.

Father, give me persistence and patience for each challenge I face today.

69

A MARKET PROBLEM

During a phone call with Churchill Mortgage managers across the country, my favorite moment was when one of our leaders in Texas recounted a conversation he had with his coach. While acknowledging that the housing market at the time was difficult in many ways, statistics by almost every measure showed that the market was favorable and ripe with opportunity.

"It's not a market problem; it's a doing the work problem," the coach said.

If you want to win in in a challenging market, or any season for that matter, you have to double down on the right activities and do them consistently over time. While there are many innovative ways to deploy these activities, it comes down to:

- getting in front of more people,
- having something of value to deliver,
- serving others.

When I look at the most successful people in any industry, they are the ones that do those three things best.

But wisdom is shown to be right by its results.

LUKE 7:35

When it comes to success in business, there is a new program or gimmick almost every week that promises supernatural results. It is much like the weight-loss industry. The facts are, however, that it has been proven, with few exceptions, that eating healthy, eating less, and exercising more produces the result. That is wisdom.

With your business, remember that while there are many new and interesting ways to do it, the bottom line is that if you want to grow, you need to get in front of more people, be able to deliver something of value to them, and provide a level of care they remember.

One more thing—in whatever you are trying to achieve, observe the most successful people around you today. Study what they are doing and commit to doing that work. It is not easy, or always fun, but their results can provide a playbook to follow.

Wisdom is shown to be right by its results. Follow the result, not the excuse. It is not a market problem. It is a doing the work problem.

Father, give me the wisdom to know which steps to take to increase my business today and the discipline to do the work.

70

ENDLESS FOUNTAIN OF WORDS

Sometimes, a quick weekend trip is all you need to recharge. Since I didn't want to compromise the workday, I booked the last flight out. As Susan and I were leaving the office, we checked on our flight to find that it was delayed.

Once at the airport, we decided to snag some dinner. By the time the food *finally* came, we heard our gate had changed to the other side of the airport. So, we scarfed it down, headed to the new gate, and waited, only to be delayed again.

After boarding the flight, we found two seats near the rear with a little extra room. It was already past our bedtime, so we looked forward to catching some Zs. No luck. Someone decided the window seat next to us was the best option.

But that wasn't the worst of it. I don't know why God blesses some people with a fountain of words that never runs dry, and I'm equally confused as to why he allows the devil to choose for those people a voice that runs up my spine, but he does. And she was sitting right in front of me. Needless to say, we didn't get any sleep.

At the car rental counter, we found ourselves at the back of a long line. Remarkably, the girl who was in front of us on the plane was immediately behind us, and she still had plenty of words left!

When we finally made it to the counter, we discovered that our reservation was only a suggestion. The kind man suggested that if I wanted a car, I should try another company. I did, and it was only twice the cost!

How you choose to live in the gap between expectation and reality has a lot to do with where you place your hope and trust.

But with God everything is possible.

MATTHEW 19:26

Things rarely go according to plan, but if you remain flexible and kind to everyone, it can still be a great trip. Today, when things catch you off guard, remember that you can only control yourself. Let God guide you through those moments, and find reasons to be kind and grateful. Life can be a bumpy ride. Let the Holy Spirit ride shotgun, and enjoy it!

Holy Spirit, fill me with love and grace for my journey today.

71

STOP FIXIN'

I've lived in Nashville for twenty-seven years, and I finally feel like I am beginning to fit in. Since I am from Massachusetts, what Southerners refer to as a Yankee, I had to learn Southern words, sayings, and dialect so that I could effectively communicate.

One phrase I had to work hard to understand is "fixin' to get ready." It is an adorable little diversion that basically means, I know I need to do something, but no action has taken place. In other words, all talk and no action.

We all have things we talk about doing, but don't take the first step to do them. We set a goal, and that makes us feel good momentarily, but it forever remains a wish rather than a responsibility. We go to seminars or conferences to learn new ideas or get motivated to implement a strategy, but we don't execute it. We just talk about it.

So you see, faith by itself isn't enough. Unless it produces good deeds, it is dead and useless.

JAMES 2:17

It's the same with our faith. Faith without action is useless. It is just chatter, like the set of wind-up chattering teeth I loved as a child. They moved at a steady pace but never chewed anything. They were interesting, but useless. I cringe at how many times I have told God I was going to do something, and he knew better. He likely just snickered with a celestial eye roll and showed me grace.

Where do you need to move from wish to action? From hope to discipline? From promise to production?

Here are few thoughts on how to shift the ledger:

1. Write down your responsibilities.
2. Be real with yourself, prioritize, and make sure you are willing to sacrifice what it will take to accomplish those responsibilities.
3. Tell someone what you have purposed. Invite accountability.
4. Get started. Stop making excuses and act.
5. Recommit daily until the task is complete or the new behavior created. Consistency is key.

Stop fixin' to get ready. Execute. This is critical both for your own progress and for your relationships with teammates, customers, family, and most importantly, God. Let your production define you, not your promises or pronouncements.

Father, free me from the bondage of procrastination. Give me the discipline to act.

72

A GOOD REPUTATION

We were in the Delhi airport, exhausted after barely sleeping on the fourteen-hour flight. A little nauseated, fussy, and completely confused, we had to find our way to a connecting flight to Bhubaneswar, and, well, we couldn't read the signs or understand how to communicate clearly enough to get advice.

As we scurried around like rats searching for cheese in a maze, we finally found someone in a uniform (not sure what type of uniform, but we thought they must know something). He stopped what he was doing, listened to us, and read our tickets. But he didn't just tell us where to go (he knew we were incompetent). Instead, he walked us all the way through the various checkpoints and to our gate. It's hard to explain the relief we felt. The uniformed stranger brought hope where there was no hope, and it made all the difference.

Never let loyalty and kindness leave you! Tie them around your neck as a reminder. Write them deep within your heart. Then you will find favor with

both God and people, and you will earn a good reputation.

PROVERBS 3:3–4

H.O.P.E.—Help One Person Every day.

Helping others is one of the few things that proves the law of reciprocation. The measure of hope you receive will be directly equal to the measure you give. The scales never seem to be exactly in balance on this, but over time, it evens out. Some days you may feel that all you do is help others and wonder who is there to help you. Other days, you might feel like you just don't have anything to give and need others to carry *you*. However, if you make it a priority each day to find someone to help, opportunities, joy, and hope will flourish in your life.

Help one person every day. This simple practice, along with loyalty and kindness, will lead to favor with God and with other people, earning you a good reputation. And who doesn't want that? Someone nearby is completely lost and in need of your support today. Keep an eye out for them!

Father, open my eyes and heart to those in need of hope today.

73

HEARTBREAK HILL

The Boston Marathon is one of the most storied and difficult marathons held each year. In running circles, winning that race is like winning the Masters in golf, the Super Bowl in football, or the semi-annual Ping-Pong tournament at Churchill Mortgage.

It is a punishing run with the most difficult stretch, Heartbreak Hill, occurring around mile twenty. By itself, that half-mile incline is a difficult run, but tackling it toward the end of the race after already covering twenty miles is a challenge that makes runners want to quit, wrap themselves in tin foil, and go to the pub for a cold beer. For those who endure that final, punishing test, however, the Prudential building comes into sight, followed by a short downhill run to the finish line.

No matter the challenge, the toughest stretch always happens right before the most significant accomplishments. Similarly, heartbreak typically precedes the most joyful moments. It can be confusing, frustrating, and move people to a breaking point instead of a breakthrough.

Jesus replied, "You don't understand now what I am doing, but someday you will."

JOHN 13:7

Heartbreak manifests itself in many ways. The week before every mission trip I have ever taken, huge distractions and troubles hit the mission's team, as well as my own life, causing people to pull out or seriously doubt going. Even during the most joyful seasons, so many people deal with heartache, sickness, disappointments, and troubles of all kinds. When things turn extremely difficult in business and questions outnumber answers, anxiety spreads like a plague.

I read that you don't really begin to train until you go as far as you think you can, then you force yourself to take another step. Evil always tries to interrupt good and take your eye off what is most important. Whatever heartbreak hill you are on, keep going. Don't quit on yourself or others. You will get to the top of the hill and hear the victory band playing. Don't give up.

Father, I don't feel like I can take another step. Give me the strength and courage to tackle my Heartbreak Hill.

74

TETHERED OR NOT

March 1993. South Padre Island, Texas. A twenty-two-year-old, a 150-foot crane, a bungee cord, and fifteen friends. What could go wrong?

I was a senior in college and determined to make the most of my spring break trip. One morning, my friends and I spotted a glorious structure stretching out over the ocean as we were walking to the beach. The sign beneath it invited people to pay a bunch of money to climb aboard, strap a rubber band to their ankles, be lifted 150 feet in the air, and jump off with the promise that the bungee cord would stop them from hitting the hard ground beneath the water. Brilliant!

In that moment, the only thing greater than my fear of heights was my ego, so off I went. As the crane started lifting, my knees buckled and I stiffened in fear. During the never-ending ascent, the thoughts inside my head were a mixture of a verbal beat down for allowing my pride to cause me to do something dumb and pure terror. Internally, I was weeping like a child.

Then the crane stopped and swayed slightly back and forth in the breeze as if waiting for my decision. Do I have the courage to jump? Should I just have the crane take me back down? I inched toward the edge of the platform, closed my eyes, and leapt.

Let your roots grow down into him, and let your lives be built on him. Then your faith will grow strong in the truth you were taught.

COLOSSIANS 2:7

Much of our lives are spent stuck in between two choices: In one direction, there is a thrilling opportunity with risk involved. In the other, the path back to safety beckons. Should I take that job? Can I risk getting hurt in another relationship? Am I capable of pulling this off? But you don't get better without getting uncomfortable.

Sometimes, God calls us to take a risk. If we properly tether ourselves to his Word and promises, however, we can leap with confidence, knowing that even if we fail, he will restore us.

Is God calling you to leap out into the unknown? If so, he is waiting for you there.

Father, help me trust you and obey you courageously.

75

A VERY TASTY DISH

When I sat back down, I was pretty darn proud of myself. Someone needed to say something, so I did. I got up, went over, said what I thought needed to be said, and sat back down. Justice was served and we could move on. The next several minutes, however, were torture.

I wish I hadn't said it that way. Why was I such a jerk? They have every right to do what they are doing. Just because I don't like it, doesn't make it wrong. I shouldn't have said anything at all.

And finally, *You need to apologize.*

I got back up, walked back over to the person I had self-righteously "straightened out" a few minutes before, and attempted to mend things with a humble apology. They thanked me and we had a few minutes of very pleasant conversation.

Let your conversation be gracious and attractive so that you will have the right response for everyone.

COLOSSIANS 4:6

I'm obviously a dense student in some subjects because this is a lesson I have had to learn repeatedly. Too often, my mouth outruns my brain with my heart finishing a distant third. When my heart finally does catch up, it reminds my brain that it was ill-advised and my mouth to swallow some pride.

The next time *your* mouth outruns your heart and brain, do the next right thing. Humble yourself, admit you were wrong, and show some integrity by apologizing. Having the right response to people by leading with meekness instead of pride is relationally attractive. When your response is supercharged with grace and kindness, it can turn conflict into friendships.

When you find your mouth getting ahead of the rest of you, like mine often does, do your best to slow down long enough for your heart to catch up, or you may find yourself perfecting the art of doing the next right thing. There is a silver lining, however. Eating some humble pie and apologizing is a very tasty dish when prepared from the heart with love for both God and your neighbor.

So, go ahead, season your conversation with kindness and grace. It will go a long way in helping you prepare the right response for everyone.

Father, slow me down. I want my words to build others up instead of tearing them down.

76

THE RIGHT MEASURING STICK

There is a little town in central Alabama called Sylacauga. It is known primarily for its vast resources of fine, white marble. Sylacauga is also the home of Pursell Farms, a beautiful piece of land created as a testing ground for golf course seed and fertilizer. Its founder, Jimmy Pursell, added food and lodging when he realized it would be more cost-effective to bring golf course superintendents to him to experience the results of his fertilizer instead of sending salespeople all over the country.

From there, Mr. Pursell and his family expanded the vision into a retreat center. It was the perfect location to get away with many of our Churchill Mortgage leaders from across the country to rejuvenate and spend undistracted time together.

In one of our sessions, our human resource leaders trained us on managing performance. One of the key themes was the responsibility of leaders to provide clarity and documentation throughout the journey of managing performance and not just when they are frustrated and ready to move on from a teammate.

As a leader, the most important person to evaluate is you! If a leader hasn't done their job well, they can't expect their team to perform well either.

Don't think you are better than you really are. Be honest in your evaluation of yourselves, measuring yourselves by the faith God has given us.

ROMANS 12:3

When conflict arises, I have found that the most important step in the process of reconciliation is a humble self-evaluation. I must be honest with myself first and accept my complicity in the situation. If I want to change my surroundings, the outcomes of my team, or others, I must first change myself. That begins with the recognition that there are areas in which I can improve. From there, I must change my actions.

If you are frustrated with a relationship, situation, or result, spend time in self-evaluation. Ask yourself: What can I do? How can I help? Where did I go wrong? What should I do differently? Then, take the appropriate action. Doing so will help you build team performance, positive momentum, and trusted relationships.

Father, give me the eyes to see myself clearly and the courage to make necessary changes.

77

TRANSFORMATIONAL THINKING

Belief is a tricky thing. Over time, our experiences and other people impose beliefs on us that we adopt as true. Unfortunately, they may not be the truth at all. Belief systems, however, even those based on falsehoods, are powerful. Therefore, to change our behavior we need to change our beliefs, and that means we have to change our thinking. Changing our thinking requires us to create disciplined structures in our lives that help us seek the truth and train our minds to think differently. That takes work.

When I was a freshman in high school, the varsity soccer coach said that I was one of the most talented up-and-coming players on the team. Going into that season, I struggled with a lack of confidence, which led to average results. Then, my coach imposed a belief on me that catapulted my soccer career. Once I believed I had talent, my game elevated to an entirely different level.

Contrast that to my disdain of public speaking. Growing up, I was undersized, spoke with a bit of a lisp, and stuttered out of fear. I believed that I could never be a good speaker. I carried that belief into my professional career until I could no longer hide from it. I had to create different thinking. I did that by feeding my mind with a new possibility and doing the necessary work to bring it to reality. I had to practice, observe others, get feedback, and make adjustments until I changed my belief about what was possible. Now, I love speaking in front of others.

Don't copy the behavior and customs of this world, but let God transform you into a new person by changing the way you think.

ROMANS 12:2

Transforming your life and business begins with a transformation of your thinking. It takes openness to what others and, more importantly, God tells you about what's possible.

Where in your career do you have limiting beliefs? You can break through to entirely different results if you have the courage to change your thinking.

Father, show me where I have fallen prey to limiting beliefs and help me envision what is possible.

78

A HARD SLAP ACROSS THE FACE

On September 11, 2001, I stepped out of my office to join the crowd gathered around the television just in time to see the second airplane fly into the World Trade Center. It was clear that life from that moment would be different.

I was a corporate controller for a global insurance company that sustained heavy financial losses that day. Soon after the attack, I was asked to join a team that would chop up and sell the divisions I worked for to raise capital. I spent eighteen months working exhausting hours and traveling constantly. I expected to be rewarded handsomely for my efforts and snag a great job with a different division once the deals were done. Instead, I was handed a pink slip. My services were no longer needed.

The experience reminds me of a quote a mentor once shared with me: "Wisdom is adjusting yourself to the reality of truth." Sometimes, truth is a hard slap across the face.

"For I know the plans I have for you," says the LORD. "They are plans for good and not for disaster, to give you a future and a hope. In those days when you pray,

I will listen. If you look for me wholeheartedly, you will find me."

JEREMIAH 29:11–13

The plans God has for me are not always aligned with what I imagine. When that happens, it's up to me to seek the truth and adjust to it, not the other way around.

I am too often deceived by what I want to be true, instead of accepting reality. This deficiency has trapped me in situations that I couldn't change by the force of my will, no matter how hard I tried. In those moments, my only choices were to remain stagnant in my deception and frustration or to change.

Once I got past the desire to fight for a job I could no longer have, I adjusted to the truth. It was time to find another job. I thank God every day because that loss led me to Churchill Mortgage, where my life has transformed in ways I could have never imagined.

God has good plans for you. Seek the truth wholeheartedly, adjust your life to that, and be set free.

Father, grant me the wisdom to accept the truth.

79

TRY A REGENERATIVE PROCEDURE

Both of my shoulders were shot from years of constant activity. It reached the point that I had trouble sleeping because I just couldn't get comfortable. It was painful to exercise or even put on a shirt. After listening to me whine like a squeaking door hinge whenever I moved my arm, Susan pushed me to do something about the situation.

Since I wanted to avoid surgery at all costs, a friend who is a personal trainer introduced me to a sports medicine doctor who specializes in regenerative procedures. His practice uses platelets and stem cells instead of knives and stitches to fix broken places.

Basically, they remove your own blood and/or marrow, spin it to extract what they want, add some magic formula, and then inject it back into the problem areas.

The potion goes to work, regenerates the tissues that were shredded, and voilà! Like new again. Admittedly, the process was painful, but only temporarily, and I was up and running in no time.

And I will give you a new heart, and I will put a new spirit in you. I will take out your stony, stubborn heart and give you a tender, responsive heart.

EZEKIEL 36:26

Sometimes we need God to do a little regenerative surgery in our lives. We need his help to remove negative thoughts, habits, and, sometimes, even people. Then we need him to find something better and inject it into our lives to promote growth, healing, and a more productive future.

Years ago, my friend Cindy Ertman taught me how to dynamically change my direction. She said to pick three things to stop doing and three things to start doing and then get to work on both. In other words, remove the bad and inject the good.

The good news is that what you need to promote growth and a future is already in you. You just need to ask God to help you pull it out, clean it up, add some good stuff, and put it to work. Sure, it can be painful for a moment, but it's worth it. Don't wait until the pain is too great to function. Start your regenerative process today!

Father, I need you to do a healing work in my heart. Take away anything that doesn't glorify you, and make me new.

80

PARTY ON A PONTOON

We have an acronym around our office. API: assume positive intent. When we look for reasons to understand and accept others and to give them the benefit of the doubt, relationships flourish, people draw closer to each other, and problems get solved. Conversely, when we consistently look for reasons to be offended, find fault, or take a personal advantage, relationships crumble, divisions deepen, and problems are exacerbated.

Throw out the mocker, and fighting goes, too. Quarrels and insults will disappear.

PROVERBS 22:10

In Hebrew, the original language of Proverbs 22:10, for the word mocker is לץ (*lûṣ*), which can also mean scorner or scoffer. When we look for this word elsewhere in the book of Proverbs, a sobering picture evolves. A mocker is arrogant and self-centered, or self-important. He is dismissive of understanding and often causes strife through his ridicule and contempt for others.

Proverbs 9:7–8 warns against even attempting to show a mocker the error of his ways because doing so only invites injury, insult, and hate.

We've all been around people like this, and it is always unfortunate, especially when it happens within your team or family. It is lamentable, because most mockers have valuable, redeeming qualities, but their weaknesses are profoundly destructive. They always seem to leave a negative emotional wake behind them.

In contrast, people who are uneasily offended and who try to understand others and assume the best of them tend to float through life on a pontoon full of friends and opportunities.

Susan says that if you look hard enough for something, you're sure to find it. That's wisdom. If you want more peace and joy in your life, start looking for it. Give people grace and focus on understanding them rather than being right. The law of reciprocation applies here for sure. The measure you get will be directly proportional to the measure you give.

Avoid being burned by your own flames of arrogance, ridicule, and strife. Douse the fires around you with a little API instead, and watch your impact and relationships flourish.

Father, make me a peacemaker instead of a scoffer. Help me live and lead with the assumption of positive intent.

81

TOSS THE MONKEYS OVERBOARD

I have always considered Wednesday the single most important day of the week. Smack dab, right in the middle of the week, it fully transitions you out of Monday, sets you up to finish another week strong, and brings the weekend into focus.

Well, then again, maybe Monday is the most important. Win Monday, and you win the week. Monday is a chance to start strong and get a leg up on the competition. Yeah, definitely Monday.

What about Thursday? Yup, Thursday is the most important day in the mortgage business. It is the day to set your clients and partners up to find houses over the weekend and give them the confidence they need to write a contract. It is a great date night, as well.

Okay, the most important day of the week is . . . today

There are a lot of things I want to accomplish each year. Some are important goals I have for a particular season of life. There are things I want for my marriage, family, business, and team. There are problems to solve, parties to throw, and mountains to climb. None of it would be possible without *today*.

That is why we never give up. Though our bodies are dying, our spirits are being renewed every day. For our present troubles are small and won't last very long.

2 CORINTHIANS 4:16–17

Life has a way of piling on like a barge overloaded with shipping containers. We just keep stacking one on top of another until we are full, weighed down to the point of barely staying afloat. At work, we have issues to solve, people to manage, and meetings to attend. After work, there are baseball games, school plays, social media, and someone else's monkey. If you don't clear the deck, you're gonna sink.

The Lord promises to renew our spirits every day. That gives me permission to take care of today because he will refill me for what I need tomorrow.

Take a little time today (the most important day) to delete some things from your calendar. Define what a win looks like for today, and make sure you have those activities lined up. Everything else will just have to wait. Clear the deck and defend yourself against other people's monkeys. Just toss them overboard!

Father, give me clarity about what is important today, and help me trust tomorrow to you.

82

RANDOM NUTS

I had an errand to run and little time to do it. Susan had been asking me for several weeks (possibly months) to take care of something, and, well, I just hadn't. Finally, I looked at my calendar, saw a time slot available and mentally committed to getting it done. I'd be a household hero, albeit a few months late.

When the time came, I scurried out of a meeting, down the stairs, and out the back door, my brain skipping from one thought to another like a squirrel running wild in search of winter rations. As I approached the storefront, I noticed a woman who kept looking in my direction. I tried to ignore her since the last thing I needed was an unplanned conversation. It didn't work. She called my name. It turns out that we were old neighbors. Reluctantly, I paused my mission. It took a few minutes to calm my frantic thoughts and be present. I very much enjoyed the short conversation.

Rush, rush, rush. When I allow my inner squirrel brain to lead, I may gather a lot of random nuts but accomplish very little. When I rush through my days, I miss *seeing* people. Rushing through work leads to mistakes. Speeding through life produces mania instead of memories. And when I forget to slow down and ask for God's guidance, I miss his best for me.

When people do not accept divine guidance, they run wild. But whoever obeys the law is joyful.

PROVERBS 29:18

Do you want in on a secret? We can accomplish more in less time if we slow down, focus on one thing, and do it well. It's true in both work and relationships.

Jesus understood this. He didn't make careless mistakes, hurry through one miracle after another checking off his divine to-do list, or tell people they weren't worthy of his attention. He took time to see them and to listen to them. And he left them better for the encounter.

Are you running wild today? Slow down. Clear some tasks off your calendar. You get to choose how to spend your moments.

Father, help me to be present and engaged so that I might be effective and impactful.

83

AN UNEXPECTED LESSON

Recently, I had the chance to experience something that I hadn't in over thirty years. My dad, brother, and I went together all the time when I was growing up and made so many great (and some not-so-great) memories. In fact, I remember learning to drive on a couple of our adventures. No, we weren't going to a ball game or the beach. We were making a trip to the dump!

After moving my daughter, Ella, out of the house she was renting, it was time to take a load to the landfill. It's shocking how much junk four college girls can collect over a short period. After taking a full U-Haul to the dump on the first go-around, I had the opportunity to make another trip the next day.

A trip to the landfill is a nasty experience, but it can also be fascinating in many ways. As I watched the bulldozers sweep by and bury everybody's garbage, I began thinking about how much stuff we collect only to toss it out when it no longer suits our needs. We seem to need things so badly that we get lost in our own excess and forget how many people in this world have so little.

For everything there is a season, a time for every activity under heaven . . . A time to keep and a time to throw away.

ECCLESIASTES 3:1, 6

From the very beginning, God knew there would always be people less fortunate. That is why he called on us to provide for them. I love that today's Scripture reading begins with a call to work and then follows with the call to give. We are called to take care of our families instead of waiting for someone else to do it. Once we have done that, then we are in a position to care for others.

Getting rid of our trash physically, relationally, and emotionally is an important part of living a productive and uncluttered life. The work can be unpleasant, but it's worth it. The process is also a great reminder to say no more often on the front end—to both possessions and people—to free up space and resources to help those in need.

What do you need to let go of today?

Father, help me let go of all that no longer serves me so that I can more fully be a blessing to others.

84

THE 80/20 RULE

As a part of my routine each morning, I spend time reading, writing, praying, and exercising. I figure that if every day starts there, it's going to be a pretty good day.

Sometimes, I combine the writing and praying by journaling. Recently, I was writing down the names of several people who were on my heart and prayer list when I got to one named Mike. I have a lot of Mikes in my life, so I immediately said, "Wait, I need to put his last name so God knows who I mean." That's when one thought made me laugh and the next smacked me upside the head.

First, I thought, *How crazy of me. God knows my heart and thoughts. He doesn't need the last name; he put it there!*

Secondly, I was reminded to spend less time talking and more time listening for God's response. I often spend all my prayer time talking to God and very little time asking questions and listening. And as a Maori proverb states, "The first stage of learning is silence; the second stage is listening."

Understand this, my dear brothers and sisters: You must all be quick to listen, slow to speak, and slow to get angry.

JAMES 1:19

Growth requires putting our mouths on pause and activating those funny-looking things on the sides of our heads. Most people are afraid of the silence, and, therefore, fill it up with a constant noise that blocks the process of hearing, learning, and trusting. If you want to influence people, learn to ask great questions, and then shut up long enough for them to answer. Allow the silence to reveal truth and connection. Here's the catch: you have to care enough about the person and their answer to wait for it.

The 80/20 rule applies to trusted conversations. It means you listen eighty percent of the time, while only speaking twenty percent. Most people have it the other way around. As author and motivational speaker Todd Duncan teaches: talk less, sell more.

What have you missed hearing because your words, both those inside of your head and those coming out of your mouth, are blocking your ears? Are you more focused on being interesting or interested? Imagine a prayer life with the 80/20 rule. Yeah, that makes me nervous too.

Father, help me be quick to listen and slow to speak.

85

L.I.V.E

I once had a conversation with one of our leaders in which we were discussing a growing frustration with a teammate. This teammate had unquestioned intellect and ability. He was likeable too! The problem was that he seemed unable to listen. He was far more concerned with telling everyone what he was doing instead of listening to what others were trying to say. Sometimes, he even offered irrelevant solutions to a problem the team was facing before he knew the facts or understood the issue. His self-focus was chipping away at the rest of the team's trust in him.

A fool's proud talk becomes a rod that beats him, but the words of the wise keep them safe.

PROVERBS 14:3

When we are too proud or insecure to listen, we slowly remove ourselves from the solution without even realizing it. Fancy words and boastful comments may sound good in our heads, but they repel teamwork and slowly cause people to stop even trying to hear us. We earn the right to weigh in on other people's problems by showing them we care about them. And they know how much we care not because we can solve their problem, but because we *listen*. Active listening is a skill which we all need to improve.

Here is one technique I have learned that helps: before you think about talking, recite the last letter in the last word spoken by the person with whom you are speaking. This forces you to listen with an intent to hear rather than respond. It also helps to ask yourself a clarifying question, such as, "What problem are we trying to solve?"

I have found that the acronym L.I.V.E. is a great way to remember how to approach important conversations at work and in life:

- Listen to others.
- Involve them in working toward a solution.
- Validate their insights.
- Execute a plan together.

Entering a conversation with a solution without first listening to the problem is just foolish. It kills teamwork, too. Don't let your pride get in the way of all you are attempting to achieve.

Enter every conversation with a commitment to listen. That is how a high-performing team succeeds.

Father, make me quick to listen and slow to speak.

86

A SLEEPLESS NIGHT

There are nights when I have so many anxious thoughts racing through my brain that I just can't sleep. When this happens, my default coping mechanism is to pray. Often, this means turning my heart to Psalm 23. Usually, after silently praying it a few times, my mind relaxes and I drift off to sleep.

One night, however, the Twenty-third Psalm itself was a source of conflict for me. "The Lord is my shepherd; I shall not want" (NKJV).

Wait a minute. I do have wants and a lot of them. And am I really living my life as a sheep in need of a Shepherd, or am I just another wolf in sheep's clothing, going about life in my own way as I try to satisfy those wants?

This conflict kept me up for quite some time. I then shifted my thinking to checking the motives behind my desires, and I came to a conclusion: it is okay to want.

I want good health for my wife in every way. I want healing for a sick friend. I want financial security for my family and for us to live in harmony. I want my business to be successful and my teammates to live great lives. I want to feel, and be, my best.

If you think you are too important to help someone, you are only fooling yourself. You are not that important. Pay careful attention to your own work, for then you will get the satisfaction of a job well done, and you won't need to compare yourself to anyone else. For we are each responsible for our own conduct.

GALATIANS 6:3–5

We all have desires. The purpose behind them and the integrity with which we pursue their fulfillment are what count. Resist self-absorption and find ways to help others. Own the responsibility to be your best. Do the work God gave you with excellence.

When my desires are fueled by good motivations, they create a passion to do great work. When I combine that with the humility necessary to seek guidance, those around me benefit. And it benefits me too. When I go it alone, I end up in a dark valley, but when I allow my Shepherd to lead me, my cup overflows with blessings.

Father, lead and guide me. Fill my desires with good things.

87

PRIDE BEFORE THE FALL

Uzziah was only sixteen years old when he became king. His father, who reigned for almost thirty years, did a nice job growing and protecting the kingdom until he took his eye off what was most important. This resulted in an uprising against him, ultimately ending in his assassination. Nonetheless, the people crowned his sixteen-year-old son, Uzziah, as the next king.

It must have been overwhelming to become the supreme ruler of a kingdom at sixteen. I wasn't even supreme ruler over my school locker at sixteen. If it didn't involve a ball or a girl, it wasn't getting my attention.

Amazingly, Uzziah did a marvelous job for more than fifty years. He rebuilt towns, improved infrastructure, invested in national defense, and led his people to victory in battle. He was the second-longest-reigning king in the nation's history and became very powerful.

By all accounts, Uzziah took the kingdom of Judah to the next level. But then his humanity got a hold of him.

But when he had become powerful, he also became proud, which led to his downfall. He sinned against the LORD his God.

2 CHRONICLES 26:16

It's always painfully true that pride comes before the fall (Proverbs 16:18). When we start to enjoy the mirror more than the "Book," bad things happen. Uzziah apparently thought he was so important that the rules no longer applied to him. He began to see himself as superior to others and above God's laws. The result? He was removed from power and suffered illness and isolation until his death.

Life has many cycles. Many of the difficult ones are self-inflicted by losing sight of what is most important. Without the guardrail of humility, you are just an arrogant fool heading for the nearest ditch.

Where in your life are you tempted to choose pride over humility? Have you had a measure of success and thought it was all you? Be careful not to lose sight of what is most important and all the people who helped you get where you are in the first place.

Father, give me a humble heart to protect me from losing my way.

88

BE A PURPLE COW

Today I want to focus on what makes you different. How do you stand out in the crowd?

Andy Andrews calls this your "Obvious Greater Value." Seth Godin calls it a "purple cow." What he means is this: If you are driving by a pasture full of cows and there is a purple one in the middle of the herd, which cow will you notice? Which one will you remember?

Now, what makes *you* stand out? What makes you a purple cow?

Thank you for making me so wonderfully complex!
Your workmanship is marvelous—how well I know it.

PSALM 139:14

The Bible says we are wonderful, complex creations. Each of us is one of a kind! Don't be like all the other lemmings chasing each other right off the cliff. Rather, step back, seek wisdom, and take time to think about how you uniquely bring value to others. Then, practice articulating and developing that difference.

For example, whereas most businesses simply try to squeeze every drop of energy and productivity out of their employees each day just to make the company money, at Churchill Mortgage, we prioritize people over property. This means we spend a significant amount of time, energy, and money pouring into our teammates so that their cups are full. These men and women are our most valuable assets. We don't want them to wind up depleted and exhausted. Also, at Churchill Mortgage, our teammates own our company. This means they choose to work hard because they share in the reward instead of being forced to work for someone else's gain. That makes us different.

Being able to articulate what makes you different and then committing to developing that gift is critical if you want to attract others. Being brave enough to be different than everyone else starts with your thinking.

What makes you stand out like a purple cow in the pasture? When a customer is choosing between you and all the other options, why will they choose you? Celebrate what makes you different, and then leverage those gifts for God's glory.

Father, you created me to be one of a kind. Help me be brave enough to embrace and cultivate my differences.

89

THE GOOD OLD DAYS

Their city was in a rough spot. The people had completely lost touch with right and wrong and were consumed by lewdness, sexual immorality, and all kinds of debauchery. It was so bad that God decided to wipe them from the face of the earth.

There was one man, however, for whom he had big plans. So, he sent his angels to Lot and warned him to flee with his family and not look back. In an act of reluctant obedience, Lot packed up his family into the old station wagon and headed out of town. On their way out, however, his wife lamented that she was leaving and longingly looked back at Sodom. God immediately turned her into a pillar of salt!

I focus on this one thing: Forgetting the past and looking forward to what lies ahead.

PHILIPPIANS 3:13

Oh, the good old days! We all have a definition in our heads of what the good old days are. We have times in the past when things just seemed better, easier, or more joyful. The problem is that those days are in the past and we can't get them back. We can only live in the present and work toward our future. In Ecclesiastes, Solomon also warns that it is unwise to long for the good old days.

Jesus even warns us to "Remember Lot's wife."

Business used to be easier, rates were lower, and homes were cheaper. Children used to be cuter, relationships were better, and friends were more fun. We were younger, weighed less, and were in better health. Oh, the good old days.

For some, however, the old days were not so good. Hurt, loss, shame, and regret were all in the old days too. You can't have those days back, either, and you can't change them.

You don't live in the old days. Life happens in the present. What are you going to do today to find joy and build your future? You must plow the ground in front of you. Your past has a lot of anchors that you need to pull up so that you can sail toward your future. Don't look back. Leave the good old days in the past, and press on to what lies ahead.

Father, grant me the grace to live joyfully and intentionally in the present.

90

A LITTLE CHIPPY

I woke up in a fighting mood. I don't mean that I wanted to physically pick a fight as the undersized frame and oversized mouth of my youth might. I was just a little chippy and ready to move some things forward in my business as we approached the end of the year.

As the calendar year closes, most people begin thinking about their New Year's resolutions and changes they want in their lives. It is a perfect time for the dogs of deception—false prophets, recruiters, news media, and the competition—to scare the neighborhood children with a lot of bark and very little bite. When that happens, it's a good day to go to battle for what you believe in.

That morning, as I was reading the Bible, a few things hit me upside the head. First, I was reminded to make sure I believed strongly in what I was fighting for and that the fight was good and right.

Intentionally choosing your beliefs is important, but it is only the beginning. You must also create the thinking and habits that allow your belief system to take root in your life.

Reflecting on this truth reminded me that I must surrender from self to God. That jab really softened me up for the next punch.

Do nothing from selfish ambition or conceit, but in humility count others more significant than yourselves.

PHILIPPIANS 2:3 (ESV)

As I read Paul's words to the church at Philippi, I realized how important it is to fight for others instead of for selfish gain. Too often, I bow up for the wrong reason.

We must carefully choose our battles and never lose sight of who we are fighting for. We don't have to worry about ourselves. When we work at helping others get what they need and desire, we typically get what we need, as well.

When I think of Jesus, who fought a very good fight for you and me, it reminds me to do the same. It is important to choose to fight for your marriage, family, teammates, business, community, and beliefs. It is equally important to fight in a way that honors God.

Don't quit when the dogs attack. Instead, align yourself with the One who promises to stand beside you until the battle is won.

Father, give me the courage and conviction to fight well.

NOTES

1. Drift Away

1. Dobie Gray, "Drift Away," written by Mentor Williams, on *Drift Away*, Decca Records, 1973, audio recording.

12. A Fist in the Air and a Head in the Sand

1. Abraham Lincoln, "First Inaugural Address" (speech, Washington, DC, March 4, 1865), National Archives, Record Group 11.

19. A Scaling Ladder

1. Robert L. O'Connell, *Team America: Patton, MacArthur, Marshall, Eisenhower, and the World They Forged* (New York: HarperCollins, 2022)

27. Rights versus Responsibilities

1. John F. Kennedy, "Inaugural Address" (speech, Washington, DC, January 20, 1961), National Archives, https://www.archives.gov/milestone-documents/president-john-f-kennedys-inaugural-address.
Chapter 54

54. Bring It About

1. Bum Phillips, Assistant Coach to Bear Bryant at Texas A&M University, 1957
https://247sports.com/coach/3616/quotes/bryant-can-take-hisn-and-beat-yourn-and-then-he-can-turn-around-35946152/

56. A Lesson in Grace from Coach Prime

1. On3, Dan Morrison, 09/20/23
https://www.on3.com/news/greg-mcelroy-addresses-death-threats-toward-colorado-states-henry-blackburn/

57. Proverbs Definition of a Teammate

1. *The Ideal Team Player*, Patrick Lencioni, May 10, 2016, Jossey-Bass